PRAISE FOR KEITH HA
ROCK-SOLID KIDS

Keith Hafner's book, *How to Build Rock-Solid Kids*, is the parenting handbook that should be handed out with each newborn child. It is simple, systematically effective, and empowering.
MASTER ERNIE REYES, *Black Belt Hall of Fame, Honored as One of the Greatest Martial Art Masters of the Twentieth Century*

I agree with the statements you have made regarding the values we need to instill in our next generation ... and what happens if we don't!
CHARLTON HESTON, *Actor*

Every now and then a book comes along which combines wisdom, common sense, and a touch of genius. Master Hafner has journalized twenty-years experience working with children into this "must-read" book for all parents. Get it!
NICK COKINOS, *Founder and CEO, Educational Funding Company*

An excellent book for young people—helping them to build character and live healthy lives! ... It's important that the martial arts can give them these vitally important values.
DR. TERRENCE WEBSTER DOYLE, *Founder, Martial Arts for Peace Association*

This book should have been published thirty years ago. I urge all parents ... teachers, and students to read and study it!
JHOON RHEE, *Martial Arts Grand Master, Founder of American Tae Kwon Do, Washington D.C.*

Rock-Solid Kids makes me think "IF"! IF I'd had this book ... while raising Ron ... there's no question that my life would have been more peaceful. No wonder that Keith's sons are where they are today. ... Congratulations on writing a book that can change parents' thinking and perhaps change millions of lives!
MASTER EDWARD B. SELL, *Martial Arts Grand Master, Lakeland, FL*

I agree with your philosophy ... for teaching parents basic child-raising skills. I know how important your work is.
ART LINKLETTER, *Best-Selling Author*

I found [your] book highly enjoyable and learned a number of things that will help in my own parenting. ... The most important thing that I took away from this book was that many of these lessons are not only for the parent-child relationship but also for the husband-wife relationship.
GILBERT UPCHURCH, JR., M.D., *Assistant Professor of Surgery, University of Michigan Medical Center*

Incredible tools! ... Should be required reading for every parent!
TIM KOVAR, *Parent of Three Sons, Sacramento, CA*

I enjoyed the book very much. The concepts are common sense ... but which are not often discussed. I'm looking forward to applying them with our kids!
DR. BILL SLICHENMYER, *Ann Arbor, MI*

Keith ... I didn't need to read your book—I've met your kids!
FRED DEGERBERG, *Martial Arts Grand Master*

Easy to read! I most like the exercises at the back of each chapter. Usually we read and forget to work with our kids. This helps to push us!
RIC VOGEL, *Ypsilanti, MI*

I very much liked reading this book. I also feel that parents have "passed on" their responsibilities to teachers and coaches. This information has direct application to my life and my child's ... as a single mom raising an eight-year-old boy!
LYNN NILETICH, *Parent, Denver, CO*

The lessons it teaches are invaluable and totally applicable to raising strong, positive, and successful children. This book lays out the "formula" in plain language! The exercises are also helpful and very clear.
CLARENCE SLAY, *Ypsilanti, MI*

This book could equally be entitled, *How to Build Rock-Solid Parents.* I think particularly of all the parents I know who are still suffering from the lack of parenting skills in the households they grew up in. Those parents especially would benefit from this very clear presentation of basic steps to successful parenting. I also think of what I know as an educator about development of knowledge, skills, and attitudes. Your book addresses each of these domains of learning. ... Clearly, this book will benefit both kids and parents. ... I know that I will use many of these suggestions and exercises in my growth as a parent. ...

SARA L. WARBER, M.D., *Co-Director, Complementary & Alternative Medicine Center Lecturer, Department of Family Medicine*

Marie and I are honored to have had the chance to review this wonderful book before it hits the "Top-Ten Bestseller List"! I think the world would be a much more positive, balanced, compassionate place if every parent or parent-to-be could read the book—once a year, at least. ... Thank you for writing your ... lessons and experiences down and making them more accessible to all those out there wanting to be the best parents they can be. It is a nice workbook, a good refresher, a reference book, and an inspirational boost.

TIM & MARIE SLOTTOW, *Parents of Three, Ann Arbor, MI*

Rock-Solid Kids is the ultimate "self-help" book! It reminds us that we have all the tools we need to raise happy, healthy kids right at our own fingertips. Self-control, respect, honesty—the ideas in the book are so familiar, yet so many people have lost sight of them. ... What I like most about your book is that it provides the means for us to do something! ... This is an interactive book that gives direction for real action. Your charts at the end of each chapter are an incredibly effective way to encourage your readers to get involved. ... Something else I like about your book is the potential benefit to both the kids AND the adults. ... It is in this way that the book is more than a guide on *How to Build Rock-Solid Kids*; it is also a guide for your adult readers to regain "Rock-Solid" values. ...

PROFESSOR ELLEN LYNCH, *Eastern Michigan University School of Business*

As an educator, I have found *How to Build Rock-Solid Kids* a good "how to" for parents and teachers. I found the text an easy read—and to the point. I especially liked your commonsense approach to child-development techniques. It is a must-read for anyone that is put in a position of child counseling. ...

DAVID DEATON, *Martial Arts Master, Hendersonville, TN*

Such an important book! I like the common language and straightforward approach. It is a practical how-to book that should benefit any parent that picks it up, reads it, and applies it. I know I have already benefited ... and so has Emma, my daughter!
CHERYL BYRNE, *Ph.D., President, Gatepower Business Communications*

Master Hafner's book showed me how to break through the barriers and truly develop *Rock-Solid Kids*!
MELANIE HAMILTON, *Parent of Two, Ann Arbor, MI*

Keith will teach you proven and easy-to-use key strategies that will help you to be a better parent.
JOHN COKINOS, *President, Educational Funding Co., Washington D.C.*

This book is awesome! Everything that I instinctively know and everything I have learned as a parent and teacher is in this book. I have already put the strategies to work with my two-year-old and my five-year-old!
DAVE KOVAR, *Martial Arts Master, Parent of Two, Sacramento, CA*

As a parent of a child with special needs, I find *How to Build Rock-Solid Kids* to be very useful in educating my child to believe in her own abilities instead of being dependent on others. I intend to use [the book] as a guide to teach my daughter the most important lessons needed to grow independently, interact appropriately, and live a positive, productive life.
KRIS KOVAC, *Parent, Ann Arbor, MI*

When it comes to raising kids, I've never seen such an uncommon display of common sense.
GRAHAM AMBROSE, *Father of Six, Grandfather of Four, UT*

[Your book] focused on many important points that most of us well-meaning parents overlook. With the changes in society and the many so-called "new" ways to raise children, it's good to read something that gets back to the values that we all should be instilling in our children. ... The exercises at the end of each chapter are quite mentally challenging. In many instances it helped inform you not what you are doing wrong, but

possibly how you can do it better. ... I would highly recommend Master Hafner's book to anyone involved with children. ...
DR. WILLIAM D. RILEY, *Ann Arbor, MI*

Congratulations! Your concise format will be well received in this busy world. Its straightforward, no-nonsense approach offers parents a good "rule of thumb" or map to guide. The clear journal-keeping format provides step-by-step progression, as well as an opportunity to review what has or what's not worked. You have offered words of wisdom and support to families. This book is a valuable tool to strengthen minds and bodies.
ANGELA ROBBEN, *Parent, School Principal, Ann Arbor, MI*

Having been practitioners, students, and instructors in the martial arts for nearly thirty years, my wife, Bronia, and I absolutely agree: This book is a jewel! Not only does it ... reach the parents of Karate students, but it [also] ... touches the minds of "KIDS." The fashion in which it was authored establishes and contributes to the positive development of "mature kids."
BOB & BRONIA SMITH, *Ann Arbor, MI*

Finally! ... A challenging book to help a parent raise children to become all that they were meant to be. Keith Hafner's "kid-ology" book can replace the need for all of the other "-ologies" that trap parents into thinking their child needs to visit one of the "-ologists" for help. Parents can use these forgotten skills to help bring their children through the different phases of their lives. ... Thanks, Keith, for presenting a Masterpiece that will develop a child in Body, Soul, and Spirit.
REVEREND EDWIN ELIASON, *Ann Arbor, MI*

I constantly hear young parents say, "Well, there are no courses to tell you how to raise children. You just have to learn as you go." Well, finally you have given them a hand. It is an excellent reference book for any parent who is concerned about the physical, mental, and spiritual growth of the children. Teachers, parents, and coaches, and anyone else involved in raising youngsters, will greatly benefit from your insight.
DENNIS BROWN, *Kung Fu Master, Black Belt Hall of Fame Member, Parent of Two, Washington D.C.*

As an educator and parent, I found *How to Build Rock-Solid Kids* to be an invaluable guide to parenting and teaching. It is a "toolbox for building strong, self-confident, and competent kids!"
BRIE STOSICK, *Educator, Parent, MI*

Over the past twenty-five years, I've taught thousands of kids and have always tried to make a difference in their lives. This book is an easy-to-read manual that will help to influence a child's attitude, behavior, and character. A "must-read" for parents, teachers, and coaches!
STEVE LAVALLEE, *Martial Arts Master, FL*

Our youth today are overwhelmed with television, video games, and computers. Keith Hafner's book, *How to Build Rock-Solid Kids*, gives parents and teachers hope ... and a format to teach kids in a powerful, positive way.
GREG TEARNEY, *Martial Arts Grand Master, NY*

How to Build Rock-Solid Kids is a "hands-on" tool that parents, teachers, coaches, and educators will find easy to read and implement. It is a logical, step-by-step guide that will improve the attitude, spirit, and well-being of not only the child but [also] everyone that is involved with that child's daily life.
JOYCE SANTAMARIA, *Martial Arts Master, NY*

When it comes to generating results in the lives of children, Keith Hafner is a proven authority. With decades of experience and thousands of graduates, Keith has the knowledge it takes to create a wonderful program for guiding children to the success that is the potential within every child.
STEPHEN K. HAYES, *Ninjitsu Grand Master, Black Belt Hall of Fame*

After twenty-five years teaching children—it's exciting to finally discover a book that combines the scientific with the practical. ... I ... plan to recommend the action formulas to every parent I know. The contents are simple without being simplistic and powerful while being easy to apply.
MASTER STEPHEN OLIVER, *Denver, CO*

Every parent who wants to successfully instill in their children a strong foundation of key life skills should read Master Hafner's book! These life skills are vital to ... success. ... It is a "must-read" for parents trying to raise good kids. ...

BRUCE SPIHER, Parent

Because of the unhealthy way my parents raised me, I've read just about every book, listened to just about every tape program, and attended several classes and seminars on how to be a great parent. I felt like I had a pretty good handle on how to raise my kids. I was hesitant to invest the time to go through your book. But as I began to read it, I was beginning to feel a recommitment growing inside of me—to not only be a great dad but [also] on how to raise my kids so [that] they can be confident. ... Your book gave me the insights and tools I needed to take my parenting beyond just being a great dad. ... So I thank you, Master Hafner, for inspiring me to dig a little deeper, be a little better, and to raise my standards higher. I highly recommend that all parents get their hands on a copy of this book. Whether you think you're a great parent or you think you need some work, this is the finest book on the subject ever published!

BRIAN K. VOILES, *Father of Four, UT*

Having an action plan to meet our parental goals of guiding and leading the development of our children to a productive life is crucial. Keith Hafner presents his action plan.

JIM HARKEMA, *Former Football Coach, Eastern Michigan University*

How To Build Rock-Solid Kids

How To Build Rock-Solid Kids

12 Proven Foundation Stones
Every Kid Needs For
A Rock-Solid Future

Keith Hafner

KEITH HAFNER'S KARATE • ANN ARBOR

Keith Hafner's Karate
214 S. Main Street
Ann Arbor, MI 48104
khafner@provide.net
734-994-0333

ISBN: 0-9703577-1-0

Printed in Canada

CONTENTS

FOREWORD

Do Keith Hafner's "Rock-Solid Kid" strategies work? Sure they do! We're Jason and Ian—Keith Hafner's sons. You'll see our names often in the upcoming pages.

Our dad used these "Rock-Solid" strategies to raise us. Dad was always working on something: advising us, coaching us, challenging us, listening to our ideas, helping us with our goals and plans. In fact, many exercises you'll find in this book were developed just for us! So yes, we were Dad's guinea pigs!

Was it easy? Not always! But even at a young age, we knew we were being "groomed" to be something special.

For instance, in our earliest recollections, Dad was already telling us, "You guys can do difficult things." And, "You can do anything you set your mind to." And, "Never worry about what your friends are doing—you're Hafners. We do things differently." As we grew older, he would tell us, "Someday, guys, when either of you walks into the room, everybody is going to say, 'There's the man!'"

We have this funny feeling that Dad's prediction has a ring of truth. How come? That's what they say when Dad walks into the room!

Yet we have an even better testament about the effectiveness of these strategies. We can't wait to use them for raising our sons and daughters!

After reading this book, we hope you can't wait, either.

Jason and Ian Hafner

ACKNOWLEDGMENTS

I would like to express my gratitude to Nick Cokinos, Ned Muffley, Edward Sell, Robert Smith, and my parents, Ed and Joanne Hafner ... for all you have taught me.

To my brother, Robert Hafner, for a lifetime of friendship and support. ...

To my beloved wife, Renee, and my sons, Jason and Ian, for filling my life with love and my days with joy. ...

And to the "Audience of One"... for making a servant into a son.

Raising Happy, Healthy, Confident Kids

It's a scary world out there for kids, isn't it? Each day we ask our children to face challenges that were unheard of—just a few short years ago.

Overcrowded classrooms. Peer pressure. Violence. And levels of negativity in our society that can discourage even the brightest and most optimistic child.

But what if I were to tell you that:

1. Your children can develop the skills that it takes to be healthy, happy, and confident.

2. With the information in this book, you can teach them yourself.

3. Your kids will enjoy the process!

No fancy theories or big words, either—just good old-fashioned common sense.

Long before parents began expecting school, therapy, and drugs to do the job for them, parents taught these skills in the home. And now, with these simple strategies for building "Rock-Solid" kids, you can, too!

For more than twenty years, I have been researching the answer to this question: "*How do you raise happy, healthy, and confident children?*"

My name is Keith Hafner. I'm not a child psychologist or a pediatrician. But I have worked with more than 10,000 kids in the last twenty years. It so happens that I own and operate "Keith

Hafner's Karate," one of the largest and most successful martial art schools in the United States.

My wife and I have also raised two sons: Jason and Ian. I may be biased, but they are now rock-solid young adults!

Ideas Proven to Work

Sure, it's a scary world out there. But, good news! The skills for building "Rock-Solid" kids work. And don't worry … anybody can learn and use these skills!

For centuries, generation after generation, parents have been using these "Rock-Solid" skills to raise their children. They, however, didn't have this book to help them. You do!

But we must begin now. We've only a few short years to prepare our kids before they face the world on their own.

The ideas that you will find in this book are not theories. They are proven strategies. You won't find any hypothetical ideas by some "expert" who has never worked with real kids!

In developing these strategies, I have focused on:

1. Skills that can be learned by kids of all ages—toddlers to teens.

2. Skills that any parent can teach. It doesn't require any training beyond what you will find in this book.

3. Skills that are universal and timeless. I have already successfully taught these strategies to kids from all over the world. They are not affected by time, geography, or current trends.

It doesn't matter where you live or how much money you make. They worked 100 years ago and will still be working 100 years from now.

Five Keys to Raising Happy, Healthy Kids

Before we start, there are a few points you must understand.

1. Our children's behavior is the sum of all the education, experience, and discipline that we have given them. As parents, we must take responsibility for their current state of behavior.

2. As a parent, you must accept your role as a teacher. Don't try to place this important responsibility on the shoulders of schoolteachers, Scout leaders, and soccer coaches. Teaching your child these skills is your responsibility.

And if you think you don't have time, let me ask you: How much time do you think it will take to deal with a child who is not happy, healthy, and confident? A child, for example, who suffers from low self-esteem?

You don't need formal teacher training to do this, either. Remember, parents have successfully taught these skills at home since the beginning of humanity.

3. These "Rock-Solid" kid skills deal much more with your child's success potential than the academic topics taught in school.

With these skills, all doors are open. All things are possible. Without them, no amount of formal education will overcome their absence.

Geography, Math, and English are important, of course. But have you ever met people who have achieved great academic success and were still less than successful in running their own lives? Of course you have!

On the other hand, can you imagine a child who has mastered these "Rock-Solid" kid skills—like Courage, Responsibility, and Respect—being held back by any academic limitations? Certainly not! If a child is focused, motivated, and disciplined, then he can tackle any academic topic!

4. Your child's skills will be just like yours. Your children will learn to live their lives by watching how you live yours.

Are you physically fit? Do you pay close attention to whom you associate with? Do you drink? Smoke? Do you exercise good judgment? And are you a person who tells the truth? A person who shows persistence and follow through? Are you a person who has self-control?

Your children will learn so much more from watching you than they will from listening to what you say.

5. And, perhaps most importantly—**You Can't *Not* Teach!**

Your child is like a sponge! Everything you do, and everything you don't do, teaches your child something. It might not be what you wanted to teach, but she will learn it, even so.

You'll notice that I do not spend a lot of time analyzing *why* some people are doing it wrong. I'll leave that to the "experts."

I've focused instead on the *right* things to do. I could discuss the excuses for "wrong" behavior forever. I prefer focusing on the "right" behavior and how to do it right—right now!

How to Use This Book

"Rock-Solid" kid skills present proven strategies that must be used—not just read and thought about. The strategies work, but you must work, too. Here's how.

1. Think of this book as a system, not an event. If you apply the strategies taught in each chapter and then stop using them, then your children will revert to their previous behavior. These strategies must be applied day in and day out. So much so, they become a habit. You don't even think about them to use them.

This is not a book you "finish." After you have completed the entire book, go back to the beginning and start over.

Think of the skills your children will develop when they are consistently exposed to this type of training!

2. Not only is it okay to write in this book—you must write in this book! So get your pen ready!

3. Read each chapter and do the exercises with your child in the order in which they are placed in the book.

Spend a finite amount of time on each chapter. A month per chapter allows enough time to make progress.

Let's get started!

What Does Your Child Expect?

A man is moving into a new town. He stops at a gas station on the edge of town and says to the owner, "Hi. I'm moving into this town. What kind of people do you have here?" The owner replies, "Well, I don't know. What kind of people did you have in your last town?" The newcomer said, "They were awful! They were rude and went out of their way to cause trouble!" The gas station owner shrugged and said, "Well, I guess you'll find it's pretty much the same around here."

Later that day, another newcomer pulls into the same gas station. "Hi!" he said. "I'm new in town. What kind of people do you have here?" The gas station owner said, "Well, I don't know. What kind of people did you have in your last town?" The newcomer said, "They were wonderful. Everybody was friendly and went out of their way to help you!" The gas station owner shrugged and said, "Well, I guess you'll find it's pretty much the same around here."

Some people expect to find doom, gloom, and failure. Others expect to encounter kindness, friendship, and success.

You won't necessarily get what you ask for in life. Nor what you want, what you need, or what you hope for.

But you will always get what you expect.

Please understand that this is not some pop-psychology mantra. It's the order of the universe!

Is the world a wonderful place, filled with opportunities, blessings, and positive experiences? Or is it a life of hardship, filled with defeat, discouragement, and scarcity?

Whichever way you happen to believe—you are right! You create your own life experiences by the way you see your world.

To raise healthy, happy, confident children, we must develop a positive outlook. Your influence has shaped your child's outlooks, both positive and negative.

As parents, your words are very powerful. Remember, when your children are young, you are the supreme authority. Your young child takes everything you say as truth.

If you tell your three-year-old son that ... he's bad ... he'll not enjoy school ... he's not kind ... he doesn't have the skills to be popular ... guess what? He'll grow up expecting those words to be true.

On the other hand, if you tell him that he is smart, good, and fun to be around, he will grow up expecting that to be true.

Your children have no way of evaluating or critiquing what you say. Their sponge-like brains just soak up everything they hear. Without questioning, they believe what you tell them. They will expect your words to be true.

What's more, they will become true. We build our own reality based on what we expect.

I recently asked each of my two sons a question about what they remembered from when they were young. I said, "Jason, what did your mother and I bring you up to expect?"

Jason thought for a minute. Then he said, "From what I remember, you told us over and over, even when we were little, that 'you guys can do hard things.'"

Ian added, "Dad, do you remember what else you used to say? You must have told me a zillion times, 'Ian, someday when you're older, you're going to walk into the room, and everybody's going to say, "There's the man."'"

Your child has no idea what to expect in the future other than what he hears from you.

Paint a Bright Future

Smart "Rock-Solid" parents enjoy painting a bright picture of the future for their children. They are skilled at building excitement about, and anticipation for, future events. They say things like:

- "Martin, your birthday is coming up next month, and I can't wait! We're going to have such a wonderful celebration! Just think of all the fun we'll have!"
- "I know you will love school, Anita. You are so smart. You'll have lots of friends and so many great experiences!"
- "Honey, when you grow up, you are going to have a wonderful life. You will always have everything you need to make you happy!"

Smart parents are always saying positive things like this to their kids. Their children will grow up expecting positive things to happen for them. And they will happen!

Contrast this with that of the child who has heard:

- "Life is a struggle, you know."
- "It's a cold, cruel world out there."
- "I don't think you've got what it takes."

Your child will have many positive experiences in the future. And, unavoidably, some negative ones, too. So draw your child's outlook toward the positive!

Guarding the Memory Vault

You can easily apply the same strategy when it comes to remembering past events. You are guardian of the memory vault.

By reminding your children of past victories, you will give them a positive sense of the future. In doing so, you will be laying a solid foundation for future successes.

A neighbor of mine, Mr. Darcy, has two daughters, Donna and Carol. He maintains a huge video archive of their awards, accomplishments, and victories. All of their achievements, both big and small, have been carefully recorded.

Mr. Darcy is smart. He understands the value of the memory vault in reinforcing a positive outlook.

Read about the "Victory Books" on page 83 of the "Confidence" chapter? I got the idea from a mother I know. She keeps scrapbooks and photo albums filled with a record of every victory or success that her children have experienced. She is quick to pull out the book and remind her kids of all the wonderful things that have happened to them.

Compare this with the father who always seems to remember only his daughter's shortcomings. He says things like:
- "You were never very good at sports, were you?"
- "Remember that time I got the call from school, saying you were failing arithmetic?"
- "You were always quite a handful when you were little."

You guard the memory vault. You choose whether your child will remember a past filled with happy memories and successes. Or one filled with discouragement and defeat.

Word Choice

Word choice is another key factor in developing a positive outlook. Words have tremendous power in shaping the way we think and feel. With proper word choice, you can maximize positive experiences and minimize negative ones.

For example, when discussing unpleasant events in the past, use soft words. They will gently reduce the sting of a negative experience.

David might say, "I don't want to play soccer this season. I was such a dope last year. I stunk!" Then you might say, "Well, maybe it wasn't your best season. You did struggle a little."

With positive experiences, on the other hand, use big, booming success words to maximize the intensity of the experience.

You could say in Cora's presence, "Aunt Marge, it was incredible the way Cora learned to ride that bike yesterday. She was so brave, so courageous! Cora rode like an expert!"

Many people have a highly developed vocabulary for describing negative experiences. Yet have a dull, boring, limited vocabulary for describing positive ones.

When asked to describe a negative experience, they use vivid, powerful words, like:
- "It was rotten!"
- "That movie stunk!"
- "I hated that class with a passion!"

But when describing a positive experience, they use weak, boring words. They say:
- "It was fine, I guess."
- "I suppose everything went okay."

Expand your vocabulary to fit your child. Describe her positive experiences as: *wondrous, superb, terrific, incredible, awesome, enlightening, miraculous, fabulous, sensational!*

Reward Approximations of Success

To encourage a positive outlook, you must always reward approximations of success. You cannot wait until your child hits the bull's eye before you begin to praise her efforts.

Often when learning, kids won't get it exactly right the first time. They usually develop their skills over time. That's why it's important to always reward approximations of success.

If you do not reward your child's partial victories, then she will see them as defeats. She will come to expect defeat, even when she is making powerful incremental progress!

For example: Steven is four. Mom wants Steven to learn to dress himself, a big task for a four-year-old. Steven tries and tries but can only manage to get his pants on. His shirt and socks continue to be a mystery.

As the family sits down to breakfast, Mom sighs to her husband, "Well, Steven still can't dress himself."

In another home, another four-year-old, Bobby, tackles the same assignment and with the same result. However, Bobby's mom is beaming as she points out Bobby to the family, "Look! Bobby put his pants on all by himself!"

Do Steven's and Bobby's efforts represent a present defeat? Or a future victory? Which mom did the best job of getting the child to try again the next day? Steven's mom? Or Bobby's?

If you are lavish in your praise of small steps toward victory, then your child will be encouraged. As a result, she will have a much greater chance of achieving victory.

Summary.

Each conversation you have with your child plants a seed. "Rock-Solid" parents plant as many positive seeds as they can.

Each day, they look for opportunities to develop a positive outlook in their children. Then they carefully nurture those seeds. It is the accumulation of thousands of positive plantings that will make all the difference for your child.

Just never forget, your expectations of your child, either positive or negative, are contagious!

Positive Outlook Exercises

Note: Not all exercises are appropriate for all ages; choose the ones best suited for your child's age and experience level.

Week #1

1. My child has positive outlooks:	☐ Always
	☐ Sometimes
	☐ Seldom

2. An example of my child having a positive outlook:

3. An example of my child not having a positive outlook:

4. As a child, what were you taught to expect? What type of outlooks did your parents develop in you?

5. Now describe the type of future you would like your child to have. Include as many different areas of his life as possible:

6. Reread the "Positive Outlook" chapter. List here any additional thoughts, ideas, or action steps that occur to you:

☐ Check here when you have completed all Week #1 Exercises.

Date:

Week #2

1. This week, we will focus on things you are saying to your child that might influence her Positive Outlook. List here all the things you find yourself saying this week that influence her outlooks in a positive direction:	1. I said, " _____ ."
	2. I said, " _____ ."
	3. I said, " _____ ."
	4. I said, " _____ ."
	5. I said, " _____ ."
2. Now list anything that might have slipped out that would negatively affect your child's outlooks:	1. Unfortunately, I also said, " _____ ."
	2. Unfortunately, I also said, " _____ ."
	3. Unfortunately, I also said, " _____ ."
	4. Unfortunately, I also said, " _____ ."
	5. Unfortunately, I also said, " _____ ."

3. Now let's try to improve some of the less positive things you might have said:	1. Before, I said, " " .
	Next time, I will say, " " .
	2. Before, I said, " " .
	Next time, I will say, " " .
	3. Before, I said, " " .
	Next time, I will say, " " .
	4. Before, I said, " " .
	Next time, I will say, " " .
	5. Before, I said, " " .
	Next time, I will say, " " .

4. Reread the "Positive Outlook" chapter. List here any additional thoughts, ideas, or action steps that occur to you:

☐ Check here when you have completed all Week #2 Exercises.

Date:

Week #3

1. Let's begin to use some of the statements developed in Week #2 that will help paint a bright future for your child. During the next week, use as many positive statements as possible and list here the types of things you said:

2. How did your child respond to those statements?

3. How did you feel after making an impact on your child's Positive Outlook?

4. The following "positive-reinforcement" statements are somewhat weak. What would you say to "turbo-charge" them? Rewrite each statement in a more powerful, high energy way. Don't be afraid to be a little outrageous in your choice of words.	1. "You did a good job on the lawn."
	2. "I liked your part in the recital."
	3. "I'm sure you will do just fine."
	4. "We will have a nice time on our family vacation."

5. Now let's soften the impact of the following statements. Rewrite each statement in "softer" language:	1. "That was a rotten thing you did to your sister!"
	2. "Your room is a pigsty!"
	3. "You always do such a careless job!"

	4. "You never listen to what I say!"

6. Reread the "Positive Outlook" chapter. List here any additional thoughts, ideas, or action steps that occur to you:

☐ Check here when you have completed all Week #3 Exercises.

Date:

Week #4

1. Continue to focus on painting a bright future for your child. When you say something to your child that reinforces that bright future, how does he seem to respond?

2. Assist your child in making a Dream List. Have him list anything and everything he would like to have, be, do, see, or experience … in his entire life! Don't eliminate any ideas because they seem too outrageous or too insignificant. Begin your list here:

3. Now transfer that Dream List to a separate piece of paper entitled "Dream List." Make two copies. Hang one up in your child's bedroom and keep the other for yourself. On an ongoing basis, direct your child's attention back to the Dream List.

☐ Check here when you have done this important step.

4. Another important part of developing a Positive Outlook is rewarding approximations of success. List six areas in which your child is required to perform. This would include things like playing on the soccer team, music lessons, schoolwork, and maintaining a clean bedroom. Then list the point at which you will provide positive feedback. Remember, begin to provide positive feedback when your child gets anywhere near the bull's eye!	1. Activity I will provide positive feedback when: 2. Activity I will provide positive feedback when: 3. Activity I will provide positive feedback when: 4. Activity I will provide positive feedback when: 5. Activity I will provide positive feedback when:

	6. Activity I will provide positive feedback when:

5. Here is a list of ways to provide positive reinforcement. Put a check beside the ones you plan to use:	☐ "Nice going, Chloe!"
	☐ "Well done, Samantha!"
	☐ Give a hearty pat on the back.
	☐ Give an affectionate hug, saying, "I'm so proud of you!"
	☐ Write a handwritten note, expressing your approval.
	☐ Tell a friend or neighbor about your child's good performance, in front of your child.

6. Now list some other ways that you plan to draw attention to your child's approximations of success:	1.
	2.
	3.
	4.
	5.

7. Reread the "Positive Outlook" chapter. List here any additional thoughts, ideas, or action steps that occur to you:

☐ Check here when you have completed all Week #4 Exercises.

Date:

Wonderful work, "Rock-Solid" parents. You have taken some important steps in securing a terrific future for your sons and daughters. I'm proud of you! Give yourself a quick pat on the back, take a deep breath, and let's move on!

BOUNDARY

Without This, You Can Forget About Mastering Any Other Skill

Self-control is the most important of the twelve "Rock-Solid" kid skills. It is also the most difficult. With self-control, you can develop any of the other skills; without it, don't even try.

Kids are born with "Rock-Solid" skills. For example, kids are born honest—they must be taught to lie. They are born confident. Otherwise, they would never learn to walk or talk.

But they are not born with self-control. Quite the opposite, in fact! As infants, we cry when hungry; we howl for attention; any discomfort prompts us to demand immediate satisfaction!

For self-control to develop, it must be taught to your child at a very early age. There is just one thing you must understand to develop self-control in your kids. It is this:

The only way for children to learn self-control is to be controlled by gentle, loving parents!

Because we are not born with self-control, we have no other way of learning. When children are very young, they must learn simple physical control. Things like controlling their arms and legs and other bodily functions.

When kids get older, self-control includes controlling actions and behavior. Older children must also learn *emotional* self-control and *mental* self-control.

Here's how it works.

*When your children are very young, when they are just beginning to move around, to take action on their own, you must immediately begin to establish **boundaries** and **rules**.*

Testing Creatures

Your ability to consistently enforce these boundaries and rules will determine your child's level of self-control.

It sounds simple enough, doesn't it? Well, it is simple. But it's not easy. Here is the challenge. While kids are not born with self-control, they are born with another interesting quality.

From the moment they are born, children are "testing" creatures. This is how they learn about the world. They are always conducting little tests. They are pushing, trying to find out what the boundaries are. Or how far they can go.

And a child who believes that the boundaries are flexible learns to disrespect those boundaries.

Let's suppose that you say to your child, "Megan, you can play in the yard but only go as far as the tree."

Here's what will happen. Megan will go right up to that tree. She is going to stand very close to the line. And when she works up the courage, she's going to step over that line.

And maybe Mom says gently but firmly, "Megan, I told you the tree was the boundary. You march right back inside that line this instant!"

Megan comes back inside the line. She has learned that the boundary must be respected. She might try it again, but sooner or later, if Mom is consistent, Megan learns that Mom means business.

But sometimes it happens differently. Megan steps over to the other side of the tree. Mom looks up and thinks, "Well, Megan isn't really hurting anything on the other side of the tree. She's okay there." Or maybe Mom thinks, "Megan is only two feet past the boundary. I don't want to make a big deal out of this," and doesn't say anything.

At this point, I'd like to remind you of an important point from our Introduction:

You can't *not* teach.

When Mom does not enforce the boundaries, Megan does learn something. It's not what Mom wanted her to learn. Mom probably doesn't even realize that learning has occurred. But Megan has learned something, nonetheless. She has learned that Mom does not mean what she says. And next time, she will push a little harder.

Please understand: Megan isn't really trying to be disobedient. She's just conducting a test. But also understand: What Mom does is very important!

If you don't establish boundaries, or if you establish boundaries and are not consistent in enforcing them, then you make it very hard for your child to learn self-control.

Children get the idea that boundaries are flimsy or flexible. So when Mom and Dad say, "No," it really means, "Maybe yes." As a result, parents end up teaching their children to disobey!

And next time, they're going to go a little bit farther. They're going to push a little bit harder. And once that process starts, it is very difficult to stop.

Three Rules Times a Zillion, Million

I believe that raising healthy, confident kids begins with self-control. So let's review the three key principles. You've got to:

1. Establish clear rules, clear boundaries.

2. Make sure there are consequences (natural or logical) for not respecting those boundaries.

3. Have consistent follow-up—a zillion, million times, if that's what it takes!

Older kids, even those who have learned self-control, may go through a period when they resist your boundaries and rules. They are still conducting tests. And now they have more will power, more ability to debate, and more desire for independence.

They will pull out all the tricks. You've heard these before:

"Mom, you are the only parent who insists on a curfew!"

Or, how about:

"Dad, you're so old fashioned! Everyone's doing it!"

Don't cave in! Even at this age, kids still need your guidance, your structure. Maybe especially at this age! Even though teens will insist that they want to be independent, they still need the security of feeling that those in charge know what they are doing.

Of course, as the kids get older, you will gradually turn the reins over to them. The key word is "gradually"!

Then it will be your turn to become a "testing" creature! Begin by giving your kids small amounts of responsibility. When they handle one task with self-control, you know that it may be okay to go to the next level. If they don't handle it with self-control, then you know that you must take a step backward.

Explain this strategy to your teenagers. Explain that their ability to handle privileges and responsibilities will earn them the right to set their own boundaries and rules—to be self-controlled.

You must occasionally remind them that this isn't just some weird torture system that you've thought up just to torment them. That's how the rest of the world works, too!

If teenagers move into adulthood without self-control, then they will have a tough time. At best, they will spin their wheels, unable to develop the ability to move forward, to achieve. At worst, they will find themselves in a position where somebody else will move in and establish control over them!

Remember, you show your love for your kids by making the tough calls. Don't give up!

Self-Control Exercises
Note: Not all exercises are appropriate for all ages; choose the ones that are best suited for your child's age and experience level.

<u>Week #1</u>

1. My child has …	☐ Lots of self-control
	☐ Some self-control
	☐ Very little self-control

2. Give an example of your child demonstrating self-control:

3. Now, give an example of your child needing more self-control:

4. Part of developing self-control is simply learning to have control of your body. Sit with your child and say, "*Dominic, let's work on our self-control. Let's try to sit completely still for one minute.*"

Describe your results here ...

Do the exercise and provide some positive feedback. Say something like, "*Dominic, you have a lot of self-control! Nice job!*"

Describe your results here ...

☐ Check here when you have tried the exercise three times in Week #1, trying to increase the time a little each session.

Date:

5. Reread the "Self-Control" chapter. List here any additional thoughts, ideas, or action steps that occur to you:

☐ Check here when you have completed all Week #1 Exercises.

Date:

Week #2

1. Setting clear boundaries is important in developing your child's self-control. List three rules or boundaries that you absolutely insist on:	1.
	2.
	3.

2. List three ways that your child challenges the rules and boundaries:	1.
	2.
	3.

3. How do you usually handle it when your child challenges the rules or boundaries?	1.
	2.
	3.

4. Continue to work on the "Sit Still" exercise. Try to increase the time that you and your child spend in the self-controlled position. Do at least three sessions and record your results here:

5. After each session, provide some positive feedback for your child. Write here the positive things you said …	1.
	2.
	3.

6. Reread the "Self-Control" chapter. List here any additional thoughts, ideas, or action steps that occur to you:

☐ Check here when you have completed all Week #2 Exercises.

Date:

Week #3

1. Continue to work on the "Sit Still" exercise. Try to increase the time that you and your child spend in the self-controlled position. Do at least three sessions and record your results here …

2. By now, the "Sit Still" exercise will have taught your child some basic self-control skills. If you see your child in a situation where she may be losing her self-control, anchor the self-controlled state of the "Sit Still" exercise by saying, nicely, "Be still." This will, in time, help your child to return to a self-controlled state. Describe your results here …

3. Last week, you listed ways that your child challenges the rules/boundaries and the ways you handle it. List here the three best ways to handle rule/boundary violations:	1. 2. 3.

4. Reread the "Self-Control" chapter. List here any additional thoughts, ideas, or action steps that occur to you:

☐ Check here when you have completed all Week #3 Exercises.

Date:

Week #4

1. As you continue to work on the "Sit Still" exercise, you can start to carry these skills over to real-life situations. To help your child see himself as a self-controlled person, after each exercise, say things like:

"You are really improving your self-control!"

2. Of course, you can also watch for different situations where your child demonstrates at least some self-control and reinforce it with this kind of statement. This week, find at least three opportunities to reinforce your child's self-control. Describe them here …

What he did:
What I said:
What he did:
What I said:
What he did:
What I said:

3. In Week #2, you listed three rules/boundaries that you absolutely insist on. Discuss each rule with your child and talk about why those rules/boundaries are important.

Rule #1:
Why it's important:
Rule #2:
Why it's important:
Rule #3:
Why it's important:

4. Explain to your child that as he matures and demonstrates self-control, his boundaries will gradually be expanded. For example, if curfew is 7 o'clock and your child respects that curfew, acting with self-control, then the curfew will eventually be changed to 7:30.

If my child shows good self-control in:

Then the boundaries will expand to include:

If my child shows good self-control in:

Then the boundaries will expand to include:

If my child shows good self-control in:

Then the boundaries will expand to include:

5. Reread the "Self-Control" chapter. List here any additional thoughts, ideas, or action steps that occur to you:

☐ Check here when you have completed all Week #4 Exercises.

Date:

---

6. Go back and reread the previous chapter, "Positive Outlook," the notes you took, and the commitments you made. List here any thoughts or questions that you have:

---

7. Excellent work! You have already begun to give your child some valuable skills. Take a few minutes right now and review your notes from all previous chapters. Write here three "reminders" to yourself:

Reminder #1:

Reminder #2:

Reminder #3:

You are now ready to move on to the next chapter!

Empower your child! Visit www.rocksolidkids.com/reports for a FREE report on teaching kids to be confident in the face of adversity!

Can Your Child Stay Focused, Even When Hit with 16,000 Messages a Day?

I know that focus is on the minds of a lot of parents. When parents enroll their kids in Karate lessons, we always ask them to tell us what the most important outcome would be. More parents say "focus" more than anything else.

Focus is the ability to direct your mental energy in a specific direction. With small children, this means paying attention and blocking out nearby distractions.

As you grow older, it means avoiding the distractions of a world of things competing for our attention, pulling us away from our goals. Show me a person who has achieved a lot, and I'll show you a focused person.

In our complicated world, focus becomes more difficult. There are simply too many choices! For example, we are bombarded with over 16,000 messages a day—all trying to persuade us to buy a particular product or point of view.

With so many choices competing for our attention, it is easy to understand why focus is so difficult. We pay attention to one thing until something else comes along that's more interesting. Then we shift our focus in a new direction.

And yet, all people, even young children, can focus. Watch a baby play with her feet. Watch a three-year-old play with LEGOs. Or an eight-year-old playing a video game.

We don't actually develop focus. We already have it. We simply need to learn to apply it where it is needed.

What Our Brains Hate

When we are young, we must learn to focus when interacting with adults. As we become older, it means focusing on what we *should* be doing instead of what we *feel* like doing.

Our brains hate focus. The human brain resists limiting itself to specific topics. It wants to be free to roam.

As I worked on the writing of *Rock-Solid*, my brain usually operated like this:

Keith: "Okay, Chapter Three, 'Focus.' Let's begin!"

After writing for a few minutes …

Brain: "Hey, wasn't that some cookout yesterday?"

Keith: "Yeah, it was, but leave me alone. I'm writing."

Brain: "No problem. By the way, did you put the charcoal away? It might rain."

Keith: "Chapter Three—staying focused. Hmm, I wonder if I did put the charcoal away."

Brain: "You would hate to ruin that charcoal."

Keith: "Leave me alone, I'm working!"

Brain: "Okay. Yessir! You're the boss. Boy, that was some cookout yesterday. … "

Three Things Kids Need to Stay Focused

Focus is important for your children because without it, they miss out on a lot of learning. They simply don't hear the things they are meant to hear.

When kids are little, they must learn to focus within their immediate surroundings. For example:

1. To stay focused on assigned tasks until completed.

When my younger son, Ian, was little, he was given the task of cleaning his room. He would have the best of intentions until he picked up the first toy that caught his eye. Then he would be totally focused on playing with that toy.

This is completely normal for a young child. He merely became focused on something that was more interesting than the assigned task.

Our job, as Ian's parents, was to gently redirect his focus back to the task at hand. A child must be taught to focus on things that are important, not just things that are interesting.

2. To listen effectively, making simple eye contact.

Five-year-old Noah, for example, couldn't maintain eye contact. Worse, he would add unrelated things to a conversation or simply walk away. Even though Noah was smart, he didn't appear that way to most people because of his lack of focus.

3. To think about a specific topic for a sustained time period.

Martin was four years old when his mother, Bethany, decided to work on his focus. Martin didn't seem to have much focus when it came to conversation or looking at books.

But Bethany did observe that when playing with LEGOs, Martin would become totally absorbed. He would often stay focused on that activity for thirty to forty-five minutes at a time.

Bethany reasoned, "Martin has focus—we just need to work on applying it to other areas." Bethany bought a couple of workbooks, "Math for PreSchoolers" and "Phonics for PreSchoolers."

She then conducted a test. She found that Martin would pay attention for about seven minutes before he got bored.

Bethany continued to work in the study books with Martin each day. When he began to lose focus, she would gently try to direct him back to the books.

She would say things like, "Let's stay focused for a couple more minutes, then we'll do something else."

Or, "Let's see what's on the next page."

Bethany was smart. She knew not to try to force focus on Martin. When Martin did reach his focus limit, she would let him end the session.

Bethany kept track of how much time they spent in each session. She marked on the family calendar the number of minutes they spent. She did this each day, never forcing Martin—just letting his natural "LEGO and cartoon" focus move into the workbook study. Soon, the "7's" and "8's" she was putting on the calendar began turning into "12's" and "13's." After a few weeks, Martin could pay attention for up to thirty minutes at a time.

Focus in Depth

Focus is also important because it is the long-term pursuit of a subject matter that is valuable.

When you study a field in depth and move to a higher level, you change. You take on those higher qualities of excellence.

Many parents today want their kids to experience as many things as possible. They want their kids to be well-rounded. The problem is, the kids never pursue any one subject in-depth.

These children jump from activity to activity, never really scratching the surface, never finding the personal benefit that comes from focused study.

For example, Max and Oscar both started tennis lessons at the same time. As beginners, they made good progress. When the class was over, Oscar enrolled in the intermediate class. Max, however, just wanted to move on to something else.

As Oscar stayed focused on tennis, his skills continued to develop. He no longer felt like a beginner. He even decided to take the advanced class when it came time.

Because of his focus, Oscar was learning to be persistent, to set and reach goals, and to overcome discouragement. These skills will carry over into other areas of Oscar's life. He can stay focused when pursuing other types of goals, too.

Max, on the other hand, moved on to golf and later to ice hockey. He was always stuck at the beginner level because he hadn't learned to focus on specific areas.

Max loses focus when an activity becomes hard. He moves on to a new activity. He has developed a pattern of moving from activity to activity, never advancing beyond the beginning level.

Sadly, Max will take those tendencies with him into other areas, too. Unless he learns to stay focused, he'll find it hard to accomplish very much.

Focus Comes from The List

As kids become older, focus means having clearly defined *priorities* and a commitment to pursuing them, avoiding the endless barrage of distractions.

The problem is that most kids don't *have* a clearly defined list of priorities. It's difficult to stay focused when you aren't sure what to focus on.

As adults, we can fall into this trap, too. Maybe we ought to focus on family, but we focus on career instead. Maybe we ought to get our finances in order, but we are too focused on our social lives.

So it is with children.

They pay attention to sports when they should be focusing on academics. They are focused on friends when they should be paying attention to family responsibilities.

As they grow older, kids will earn the right to do the things they choose. To prepare them for this responsibility, you must teach them to focus by helping them establish *priorities*.

I was having a discussion awhile back with a boy named Owen, who happens to be a very focused fourteen-year-old.

He told me that his priorities were:

1. Spiritual
2. Family
3. Education
4. Fitness
5. Social.

As you might expect, Owen is a very focused kid! This clear sense of priorities makes it easy for Owen to be successful. When confronted with choices, he already knows what is most important to him. Therefore, it is easy to stay on track.

Most people can manage five to seven priorities. A typical priority list for a teenager might look like this:

1. School work
2. Family stuff
3. Social activities
4. Extracurricular sports
5. Leisure.

In my own family, our belief is that our spiritual faith in God should be our number-one priority. We have found that if we place this in the number-one position, then all of our other priorities fall easily into place.

The List versus Rollerblading

Julie, age eleven, was on the track team and was a "B" student. With her mom's help, Julie made a list of priorities and taped it on the bathroom mirror.

It read: family, school, track, friends. Julie and Mom agreed that four priorities were all that could be focused on.

One day, Julie received an invitation to try out for a rollerblading group that met Saturday mornings. Usually on Saturdays, Julie would study, then participate in family activities. Julie pleaded with her Mom to be able to join the rollerblading group.

Mom considered the rollerblade invitation. "It could work if we shifted a few things around," she thought.

Then Mom stopped. "Julie has had trouble with focus before," she thought. "That was why we made the priority list. If we add rollerblading, not only will it be a current distraction, but it also will open the door for the next distraction!"

Mom said to Julie, "Let's see if it fits on your Priority List."

As much as Julie wanted to join the rollerblading group, it was clear to her that adding it to her list would only get in the way of her other priorities.

Mom didn't have to tell Julie what to do. She just guided her into making the right decision. If they had not established a priority list in advance, then Julia would have found it difficult to understand her Mom's position.

It's also important to prepare for obstacles in staying focused. What are the distractions for your child? How can we plan to avoid them? By identifying potential distractions in advance, it makes it easier to deal with them when they occur.

How to Teach "Focus"

For example, many kids will be tempted to slide social activities above family and school responsibilities. If you can identify this type of potential distraction in advance, discuss it with your child. Prepare to deal with it ahead of time!

With young children, ages three to eight:

1. Select a project. It could be a workbook, puzzle, craft project, or similar project that requires continued study.

2. Set up a regular time to work on the project.

3. Measure and record, from day to day, how much time your child can spend in focused application.

4. Don't try to force your child's focus. If you do, then her brain will simply turn her focus off.

5. Do try to gently redirect your child's focus when her attention wanders. Say things like:

• "Let's do a little more, then we'll stop."

• "Before we stop, show me more about this part."

• "Your focus is improving. I'm so proud of you!"

6. Try to encourage attentive body language. Posture and eye contact are important ingredients of focus. Again, use gentle reminders. Don't insist.

7. You will see your child's focus gradually begin to improve. Reinforce this progress by saying things like:

• "I'm so proud of how you are paying attention!"

• "Your focus is improving—great job!"

With older children:

1. Together with your child, list the top five to seven priorities. Listen to your child's ideas. See if you can come to an agreement about what is most important.

2. Post the list in a prominent place—near the family calendar, for example, or on your child's bulletin board.

3. When decisions are to be made, consult the priority list. Try to coach your child into making good decisions.

Use questions like:

• "I know you want to try guitar lessons. How would this fit in with your other activities?"

• "If you do join the bowling league, how would that interfere with your commitment to the soccer team?"

If your child still wants to add an activity that conflicts with the priority list, then you will have to make an "executive decision"!

You may ask yourself, "Do I insist that we stick to our list?" Or, on the other hand, "Do I cut her a little slack and let her see for herself what will happen?"

Usually, the best answer is probably the first of these two options. However, as your child matures, you might occasionally want to handle it with the second option.

When doing so, provide a lot of supervision. You must be ready to step in if she gets too far off track.

If she doesn't get off track, she will have shown that she can stay focused, even with the additional responsibility.

Summary.

It is said that you can have anything you want in life but probably can't have everything you want. Choices must be made. Commitments must be honored. Successful living requires that you stay focused on the things that are most important to you.

Focus Exercises

Note: Not all exercises are appropriate for all ages; choose the ones that are best suited for your child's age and experience level.

Week #1

1. My child has:	☐ Lots of focus
	☐ Some focus
	☐ Very little focus

2. An example of my child being focused is:

3. An example of my child needing more focus is:

4. Three behaviors that would tell me that my child is being focused:	1.
	2.
	3.

5. Three things that are potentially distracting for my child:	1.
	2.
	3.

6. Pick an activity from the following list. You will be doing this activity alongside your child to work on focus. *Note:* If you don't see something you like, then pick any other activity that requires focus and takes awhile to complete. Try to stay away from projects that use big muscles. Select an activity that requires close-in focus. Put a check beside the activity you choose.	☐ Jigsaw puzzle
	☐ Needlepoint project
	☐ Model airplane
	☐ Craft project
	☐ Building something
	☐ Reading a lengthy book
	☐ Other

7. Reread the "Focus" chapter. List here any additional thoughts, ideas, or action steps that occur to you:

☐ Check here when you have completed all Week #1 Exercises.

Date:

Week #2

1. Begin doing the activity that you selected last week. Do three sessions, each time observing how much time your child can remain in focus. Don't do anything to try to increase the focus yet; we are simply observing and measuring at this point. Record the time spent in focused activity here.

Session #1:

Session #2:

Session #3:

2. List any other observations you have about your child's ability to focus:

3. With the youngest children, focus begins with the ability to pay attention. We control what we pay attention to with our eyes. Have your child sit facing you. You look directly into his eyes, and he looks into yours. Try to hold this for thirty seconds. Do it a couple of times. As you do this exercise, say to him, "Eyes on whom?" He replies, "Eyes on you, Mom!" How did it go? List your observations here:

4. ☐ When you want to have your child focus on what you are saying, just say, "Eyes on whom?" This will bring him back into focus. Check here when you have done this at least three times.

5. Reread the "Focus" chapter. List here any additional thoughts, ideas, or action steps that occur to you:

☐ Check here when you have completed all Week #2 Exercises.

Date:

Week #3

1. Continue doing the activity that you selected in Week #1. Again, do three sessions, each time observing how much time your child can remain in focus.

This week, try to gently extend the time your child is spending "in focus." When she becomes distracted, you might say something like, "Let's do just a little more." Or, "Why don't we do just one more chapter, then we'll stop?"

Record the time spent in focused activity here.

Session #1:

Session #2:

Session #3:

2. Last week, we worked on eye contact—an important focus tool. Another focus tool is posture. Observe your child's posture when she is in a focused state. What is it like?

Most kids' posture changes as they begin to lose focus. Observe your child's posture when she's losing focus. What's it like?

3. Practice the "posture" of focus with your child. This "posture" should include:	☐ Shoulders back, lifting the sternum, whether sitting or standing
	☐ Head held high
	☐ Muscles loose, relaxed

Rehearse this posture with your child. Practice doing it on cue. When you remind her by saying, "Posture!" she understands that it is time to do a posture check. This, along with the "eyes on whom?" exercise will give your child a couple of important focus tools.

4. ☐ When you want to have your child focus on what you are saying, just say, "Posture!" and this will bring her back into focus. Check here when you have done this at least three times.

5. Reread the "Focus" chapter. List here any additional thoughts, ideas, or action steps that occur to you:

☐ Check here when you have completed all Week #3 Exercises.

Date:

Week #4

1. Continue doing the activity that you selected in Week #1. Again, do three sessions, each time measuring how much time your child can remain "in focus."

By now, you may be seeing some significant improvements in the amount of time your child can remain in focus. This week, again try to gently extend the time your child is spending in focus. The key is to be gentle. When your child has had enough, you do not need to push him. If you do, then your child will become frustrated and immediately lose focus.

Record here the time spent in focused activity:	Session #1
	Session #2
Notice how easily your child's focus improves with these simple exercises.	Session #3

2. List some other focus-building activities that you can do with your child in the future:

3. If your child is approximately eight years old or older, she is probably ready to understand the importance of staying focused on priorities. Go back and read the priorities segment of the "Focus" chapter.

4. Now make a list with your child of the top priorities in her life. List them here:

1.

2.

3.

4.

5.

6.

Make several copies of this list on index cards. Give your child one to paste in her notebook and a couple to put up in her bedroom. You keep a copy, too. Explain to your child that you and she, together, will consult this list when new choices need to be made.

☐ Check here when you have completed these "Priority" exercises.

5. You'll have times when your child will get off track with her priorities. But if you are prepared, you can coach her more effectively. For example ...

My child will tend to put ...

Ahead of ...

When she does, I will handle it by ...

6. Reread the "Focus" chapter. List here any additional thoughts, ideas, or action steps that occur to you:

☐ Check here when you have completed all Week #4 Exercises.

Date:

7. Go back and reread the previous chapter on "Self-Control." Read the notes you took and the commitments you made in the exercise segment. List here your thoughts, progress, or questions:

Hey, "Rock-Solid" parents. Great job! Give yourself a pat on the back for completing these important chapters! You are developing true "Rock-Solid" skills. You are probably already seeing some significant changes in your child's behavior. Don't forget to continue to reinforce the skills developed in the earlier chapters. Let's move forward!

Free cassette! Call 734-994-0333 to receive a FREE copy of Keith Hafner's "The Three Skills of Listening!"

Two Keys to Respect Every Child Should Bow To

Respect is central to your child's ability to be happy and to function in the world.

The *form* of respect is shown by appropriate conduct and good manners. The *spirit* of respect is represented by a sincere appreciation of the value and the rights of other people.

We have become a very disrespectful society. You'll find many forces at work that make it hard to develop children who have respect for others. For example:

1. Some "enlightened thinkers" have told us that kids should be:
   - Allowed to make all of their own choices.
   - Allowed to express themselves in any way that they choose.
   - Treated and spoken to as if they were adults.

2. Television, especially television sitcoms, often portrays kids as having little respect for adults. On TV, kids are always outsmarting the parents while finding ways to bend or break the rules.

3. Parents are afraid, or don't know how, to insist that their children should be respectful.

Parents have heard so much of this type of thinking that they have become unsure of themselves. They are afraid to exercise their authority. Many parents tolerate disrespectful behavior from their kids that was unthinkable in the past.

This is so damaging. Not to the parents—but to the kids themselves. Disrespect also hurts the disrespector! It steals self-esteem from the person who is being disrespectful.

All kids want respect.

But they often misunderstand two things about respect:

1. You will *earn* respect in the same measure that you *give* respect.

2. You must be respectful *first*.

Why a Disrespectful Child Gets "No Respect"

A disrespectful child hurts himself more than he hurts anybody. Because he gets no respect, he turns that attitude inward, toward himself. He starts to see himself as a person who doesn't deserve respect.

It's called a *lack of self-respect*. It represents a deadly set of circumstances.

With low self-respect, a child will "sell" himself cheaply. He will fall for anything. He will never learn to hold himself to a high standard of conduct. He will tolerate all types of abusive treatment because he has no sense of self-worth.

It often happens like this:

• A kid is disrespectful, and nobody corrects it.

• Because he is disrespectful, he gets no respect from others.

• So he grows up with no self-respect.

• As an adult, because his self-respect is so low, he will accept disrespectful behavior from his own child.

• It starts all over.

We show two types of respect:

1. This is the basic level of respect due to all fellow human beings. We respect the right of other people to coexist. To pursue their own happiness and to do things in their own ways—without being robbed, beaten, or treated rudely.

Our fellow humans are all entitled to their own dignity, to their privacy, to their right to be different, and to their right to act in their own best interest.

This type of respect also includes respect for institutions and for certain things. Should you show respect for our country and its leaders? For elders and other relatives? For church and matters of spiritual faith? Of course!

How about respect for the power of an automobile? A growling dog? A sharp knife? How often have we seen somebody get in trouble because he didn't have the right amount of respect for something that could hurt him?

2. The second type of respect is one given to people who have distinguished themselves based on achievements, extraordinary levels of performance, integrity, or contribution.

This type of respect is "selective respect." It is performance-based respect, limited to the area of performance. We might respect a certain athlete, for example, for his athletic performance. This doesn't mean, however, that we would automatically respect how he conducts his private life.

Many young people make the mistake of generalizing the respect they feel toward athletic and entertainment heroes. They give them a level of respect that the personal behaviors of these heroes do not deserve.

Three Reasons Why Children Love Respect

In the martial arts, kids love respectful stuff, like saying, "Yes, sir!" and bowing. Why? Why are even disrespectful kids respectful in Karate?

1. It feels right and good to be respectful.
2. It is expected by their teachers.
3. It is not only expected. It is taught-in a gentle, friendly way.

Consider the story of Tony, a boy of fifteen whom I got to know through the martial arts.

Tony was disruptive at school and rude and inconsiderate at home. Tony had been suspended from school; he was not obeying curfews and constantly used profane and disrespectful language when talking with his parents.

Tony showed no respect for parents, other family members, or teachers at school. Not surprisingly, nobody respected Tony, either, other than a few kids at school who had attitudes similar to his.

As you can imagine, Tony's parents were heartbroken over his lack of respect. Then they heard through a neighbor that martial arts might be a good way to teach Tony respect.

When I first got to know Tony, I could tell by his appearance and the way he talked about himself that his self-respect was way down.

Apparently he saw no connection between his attitude toward others and their attitudes toward him.

Tony felt that he would begin respecting others when they began respecting him.

This isn't too surprising in a fifteen-year-old. Smart "Rock-Solid" parents understand that kids must be *taught* respect.

Although Tony was disrespectful at home and at school, he was very polite and respectful in the Karate school. He loved the protocol, the politeness of the martial arts.

I said to him, "Tony, why do you like it here?"

He said, "I dunno … I guess because of what all the teachers have done in Karate. I respect that." He added, "Plus, everybody's nice to me."

"Tony, can you see how it works? You are respected here because you are respectful."

"What do you mean?"

"Tony, would you be disrespectful here?" (His mother told me about some of the problems he'd had both at school and at home.) "Would you be disrespectful to your martial art teachers?"

"No way!"

Tony wanted, more than anything else, to be respected.

I began to show Tony how his disrespectful attitude outside the martial arts was hurting him.

Plus, how he really owed far more respect to his family and his schoolteachers than he did to his martial art teachers.

Tony began to understand. We made a plan.

1. Appearance.

"Tony, why is your Karate uniform always so neat and clean?"

"I just like it that way, I guess."

"Well, you seem to take pride in your appearance. I respect that and so do your Karate teachers."

I began to help Tony see that certain types of dress were appropriate with his friends—but were not appropriate around his family and in school. We discussed the value in taking pride in one's appearance for earning respect.

2. Language. Tony had such a sullen, negative way of speaking that people automatically interpreted it as disrespect.

What's more, he seldom looked anybody in the eye when he spoke. We began working on eye contact and a more enthusiastic voice tone.

When talking with parents and teachers, Tony would use the occasional "Yes, sir" and "Yes, ma'am." From these small steps, he was showing the grownups in his life how he was trying to be respectful.

3. Obey the "rules of the house," just as he was doing in the Karate school.

Tony had never given any thought to the fact that he should be respecting the rules of his parents' home. Yet when he came to his "Karate home," he always understood that certain rules of conduct applied.

We discussed the importance of avoiding bad language and rowdy behavior, observing curfews and all other family rules.

Tony was a good kid with some misguided thinking. He thought, "I'm not going to respect anybody who doesn't respect me." He didn't understand that you must first give respect to get respect.

When Tony began to change, his entire world began to change.

How Not to Teach Respect

Disrespect usually begins at a very young age with disrespectful verbal behavior.

Caleb began, at age three, to say "No!" to his mother when she asked him to do something.

His mom, Julie, would then begin trying to persuade Caleb to do what she wanted. She would attempt to reason with him. When that didn't work, she began to revise her request, looking for something that Caleb would agree to.

"Caleb, pick up your toys now; we have to go."

"No!"

"Caleb, we've got to get groceries and be back by seven o'clock. Please get ready."

"I don't want to go. I want to finish my TV show."

"Come on, honey!"

"No!"

"Well, just get your jacket on and let's go. Okay? We can pick up the toys later."

"I want to stay and watch my show."

"Okay, you've got fifteen minutes; then we have to go, okay?" Julie pleaded.

Of course, by now, Caleb has gained the upper hand. Unless Julie changes her approach, then Caleb's respect for her authority and his behavior will continue to disintegrate.

Now, let me ask you.

Was Caleb disrespectful by nature?

Or was he taught to be disrespectful?

Even at three, Caleb sensed weakness in his mom. She would negotiate with him—try to persuade him. Even though he was too young to understand why he was behaving the way that he was, he could not have any respect for his mom.

Remember, he is only three years old!

Respect and Kindness

When I was a kid, I was not allowed to say "No" to my parents. Disrespect was not tolerated. Maybe that's how you were raised, too.

Here's what Julie should have done from the beginning and what she still should do. When she hears that "No!" from Caleb, she should say, "Young man, you march right in there and do as you are told!"

No negotiating. No compromising. No persuasion. Just simple enforcement of authority. Like the following example.

Mrs. Dobson was growing tired of the disrespectful behavior of her fourteen-year-old daughter, Emma. Emma began to openly challenge her mother's authority. They frequently fought about family rules, dress codes, and curfews.

Emma had grown critical of just about everything: school, rules, and other people. She would always be late when getting ready. She didn't mind a bit if she kept Mom waiting for her.

Mrs. Dobson felt, at times, as though she was the kid and Emma was the parent. Mrs. Dobson hadn't intended to let this happen. However, little by little, disrespect began creeping into Emma's attitude. Mrs. Dobson had always found it easier to let the behavior slide. She would work on it later.

Lately, though, it had taken a turn for the worse. In fact, Mrs. Dobson got a call from Emma's schoolteacher, saying she had noticed some disrespectful behavior from Emma, too.

Mrs. Dobson began to realize that she had, in fact, allowed this attitude to develop. She should have caught it when it first began. Now, with a look of concern, she wondered if it was too late to do anything about it.

One day, while looking through a family photo album, she saw a photo of her Grandmother Dobson. The photo brought back fond memories of a warm and loving grandmother. Mrs. Dobson wished that Emma could have known Grandma.

Then it popped into her head. "No way would Grandma tolerate disrespectful behavior from Emma!" Grandma was sweet and kind, but you were always on your best behavior around her. You said, "Yes, ma'am," and "No, ma'am." You paid attention to your appearance. You would never think of being rowdy in her home. You would never, ever speak disrespectfully to her.

Now, Grandma was not a heavy-handed enforcer of respect. So how did she do it? She had something about her that caused you to be on your best behavior.

Grandma was a person who deserved to be respected, thought Mrs. Dobson.

Then the light went on. "So do I!" she said out loud.

Mrs. Dobson began to see that Emma had become disrespectful because she had allowed her daughter to become that way.

"Things will be different, now," she thought.

Mrs. Dobson had a long talk with her daughter. "Emma, I've messed up. I've allowed certain things to creep into our relationship that should not be there. Here's how it will be from now on … "

1. "No disrespectful talk. I am the parent. You are the child."

2. "You will not keep me waiting."

3. "Rules will be enforced. If you have questions, they must be asked respectfully."

4. "Privileges are earned, not automatic. Your privileges will be determined by your level of respectful behavior."

Mrs. Dobson stuck to her plan. Emma had no choice but to comply because Mom was serious.

After a while, Emma enjoyed the new relationship with her mother. It felt right. Grandma Dobson would have been proud!

How to Teach Respect

1. Begin by teaching your child good manners. Then insist that they always be used. Explain that bad manners will be considered disobedient behavior.

Should you require your child to say "Yes, sir?" and "Yes, ma'am?" Only if you want to raise a respectful child!

2. Show respect, yourself, to others. Don't talk disrespectfully about your boss, your mother-in-law, or your neighbor.

If your child overhears you saying, "My boss is so stupid! What a jerk!" it will make it difficult for her to not copy those attitudes.

3. Keep your word. Do what you say you are going to do.

4. Show zero tolerance for disrespect. Start when kids are small—when their disrespect is small, too. Don't let it grow.

5. Point out respectful and disrespectful behavior in others and its consequences. Disrespect hurts the disrespectful person. Show this to your kids.

Dad says to his son, "Your friend Michael is not respectful to the basketball coach. So what is the result?"

Your son says, "Coach won't play him in the games."

6. Teach that respect is earned, not automatic. It's earned by showing respect.

7. Privileges are earned by respectful behavior and forfeited by disrespectful behavior.

8. Don't just expect it—teach it! Don't just teach it—expect it! These two, side by side.

Summary.

So, "Rock-Solid" parents, tolerate no disrespect.

But remember, you might have to develop respectful behavior gradually with a lot of careful instruction.

Plant the seeds of respect early—and watch them grow!

Respect Exercises

Note: Not all exercises are appropriate for all ages; choose the ones best suited for your child's age and experience level.

Week #1

1. My child is:	☐ Very respectful
	☐ Sometimes respectful
	☐ Not very respectful

2. List some examples of your child behaving respectfully:

3. Now list some examples of disrespectful behavior that you see from your child:

4. Sometimes parents accidentally reinforce disrespectful behavior by gradually becoming tolerant of it. List some examples of times when you might have been too tolerant of disrespectful behavior:	1.
	2.
	3.

5. Now think of some ways that you might have handled those situations differently and list them here:

6. Reread the "Respect" chapter. List here any additional thoughts, ideas, or action steps that occur to you:

☐ Check here when you have completed all Week #1 Exercises.
Date:

Week #2

1. Respectful behavior begins with good manners. Put a check beside the "good-manners" strategies that you expect from your child:	☐ Saying "Yes, sir/Yes, ma'am" and "No, sir/No, ma'am"
	☐ Addressing elders by "Mr." and "Mrs."
	☐ Dressing nicely for meals
	☐ Saying "Please" and "Thank you"
	☐ Writing thank-you notes after receiving a gift
	☐ Appropriate dress for certain occasions
	☐ Using a respectful tone of voice
	☐ Following the "rules of the house"

2. List here any additional "respect" indicators that you expect from your child:	1.
	2.
	3.

3. Sit down with your child and discuss each thing you have checked. Discuss both how and when these "respect strategies" are to be used.
☐ Check here when you have completed the "Respect" discussion with your child.

4. During the next week, watch your child carefully. Don't watch for respect violations. Instead, try to "catch" your child using the "respect strategies." Reinforce them by saying things like:
- "Tyler, you looked so nice at dinner last night. Very respectful!"
- "I was so proud of the respectful way you addressed your grandmother, Christine!"
- "Dad, Simon wrote all of his birthday party thank-you notes this morning. He's becoming a very respectful person!"

☐ Check here when you have observed and reinforced your child's respectful behavior at least three times:

5. Continue to observe your child's respectful and disrespectful behavior. List a couple of examples of each:	Respectful
	Respectful
	Disrespectful

6. Reread the "Respect" chapter. List here any additional thoughts, ideas, or action steps that occur to you:

☐ Check here when you have completed all Week #2 Exercises.

Date:

Week #3

1. With your child, list people, things, and institutions that deserve our respect. List as many as you can think of here, along with the reasons why we should respect them. List also how you will show that respect.

I respect:

Because:

I will show that respect by:

I respect:

Because:

I will show that respect by:

I respect:

Because:

I will show that respect by:

I respect:

Because:

I will show that respect by:

2. Have your child pick three of the these choices and commit to doing them right away. The three are:	1.
	2.
	3.

☐ Check here when all three demonstrations of respect have been done.

3. Reread the "Respect" chapter. List here any additional thoughts, ideas, or action steps that occur to you:

☐ Check here when you have completed all Week #3 Exercises.

Date:

Week #4

1. List with your child some accomplishments he might achieve that would deserve respect:	1.
	2.
	3.
	4.
	5.

2. Next list some personal qualities that deserve respect (for example, review the "Rock-Solid" qualities listed in the table of contents):	1.
	2.
	3.
	4.
	5.

3. Talk with your child about those people who have earned respect by their achievements yet who lack the personal qualities that deserve respect. If possible, discuss a person who fits this description. How should we feel toward this person? With your child, write some thoughts about this type of person:

4. Reread the "Respect" chapter. List here any additional thoughts, ideas, or action steps that occur to you:

☐ Check here when you have completed all Week #4 Exercises.

Date:

5. Go back and reread the previous chapter, "Focus," the notes you took, and the commitments you made in the Exercise segment. List here any thoughts, progress, or questions that you have:

Well done! As you work on the "Rock-Solid" exercises, not only will you see your child's skills improving, but you will also feel your own ability to affect your child's behavior improving. I congratulate you!

WARNING: Your Child May Be Bleeding Her Confidence Dry

You watch through the playground fence. The kids are playing soccer. Your child loves soccer yet stands on the sideline, afraid to join in.

Worse, your child's self-confidence erodes even further when she kicks herself for not having the courage to act.

Now you know why self-confidence is the greatest asset a person can have. A person with confidence cuts a wide path through life. Doors open for her that remain shut for the timid. The confident person fully experiences all the excitement life has to offer!

Confidence is somewhat different from the other "Rock-Solid" skills. Here's why: *You are born with **all** the confidence you will ever need.*

Consider for a moment the way a baby develops in the first couple years of life. She moves from learning experience to learning experience. Within just one year, that helpless infant has learned to walk and talk.

Have you ever asked a five-year-old what she wants to be when she grows up? Kids always want to be the most incredible things: astronauts, professional athletes, doctors, celebrities. She has total confidence in her ability to do anything she wants.

But then something happens. Within the next four or five years, she has lost a lot of that initial confidence. She has scaled back her expectations. She's become more "realistic." By the time she's in middle school, she's lost much of that excitement about what the future has to offer.

Plenty of kids, by the time they graduate from high school, lack the confidence to get even the most basic job. How does this happen? It's an accumulation of negative thinking.

For example:

A parent tells them, "You aren't as smart as your brother."

Then they hear why: "Girls aren't supposed to be good at math."

Next the coach says, "You aren't fast [or big, or thin, or talented] enough."

Somewhere along the line, peer pressure rears its ugly head. The other kids at school start to tell your child, "Hey, it's stupid to try hard. It's not cool to do well in school. Why don't you be like the rest of us?"

It's so sad. Problem is, the negativity of today's world is contagious. It pulls people down every day. A lack of confidence is learned. You don't really have to help a young person develop confidence. You just have to keep her from losing it!

As "Rock-Solid" parents, we realize that we are entrusted with the protection of our child's self-confidence.

What can you do about it? Plenty! Let's begin.

You must understand five concepts if you are to protect your child's self-confidence.

1. Confidence is a skill, not an attitude. It can be learned, practiced, and rehearsed. If your child lacks confidence, however, it takes a firm commitment from Mom and Dad to overcome it.

Free Report! Visit www.rocksolidkids.com/newsletter and get a FREE report on how to teach your kids to resist peer pressure!

When his mom first brought Kendall to Karate, he had no confidence. He was afraid to try new things, and he avoided looking people in the eye.

His mom said, "I'm going to fight this thing! My son is smart and nice. I'm not going to let him succumb to this. I remember how I felt when I was a child and had no confidence!"

So she did one confidence builder after another. Even though, at times, it seemed that nothing was working, she stayed with it, and eventually her strategies began to work.

Kendall's confidence gradually improved. His friends and teachers noticed a difference in the way he looked and in the way he acted.

Kendall's mom was successful because of her commitment to achieving these results!

2. We have a "body language" that speaks confidence! Studies show, in fact, that how we hold our body reveals our emotional state.

You can picture how a confident person walks, can't you? Or how an under-confident person would speak?

When you picture the way that a confident person would stand, you might ask yourself:

- "Is this person standing in such a powerful way because she is confident?"
- "Or is she confident because she is standing in a powerful way?"

Does a person stand a specific way because she's scared, or is she scared because she's using weak, unempowered body language?

Well, the answer is—both! But to teach confidence, we must begin with body-language skills. Many children experience confidence for the first time when they begin to master confident body language.

Paula had been walking home from school by herself since second grade. But when fourth grade started, she changed schools. This meant that she had to walk by the middle-school playground.

Some middle-school boys always hung out at the edge of the playground. They were loud and aggressive. Even though Paula wasn't in any actual physical danger, she always felt intimidated.

When she explained this situation to her dad, he began working with her on her posture and her breathing. He also instructed Paula to look those boys right in the eye.

This eye contact was hard for Paula to learn. It took her outside her comfort zone. But Dad repeatedly role-played with her.

Soon Paula learned to use these empowering body-language techniques on her walk home. They immediately changed the way she felt. Instead of feeling intimidated, she felt confident and safe.

3. Past events also profoundly influence your child's current level of confidence—and the way you recorded those events.

Is your child's current self-image built on past victories—or failures? You must continually direct her focus toward her past victories rather than toward past defeats.

4. To develop self-confidence, you must gently and lovingly move your child outside her current comfort zone.

5. You must reinforce confident behavior, and all approximations of confident behavior, with positive feedback.

How to Teach Confidence

Take a good look at your child. How does he hold his body? Is it a soft body language? Or does he look alert and capable?

Confidence is visibly expressed through:

Posture.

Begin to work with your child on maintaining an upright posture. Lift the sternum; pull the shoulders back; keep the head held high.

Practice standing, walking, and sitting with this posture of confidence. Breathing deeply. Relaxed but alert.

Eye Contact.

Help your child become accustomed to making direct eye contact with people. Have him practice by holding direct eye contact with you. Even if he feels uncomfortable at first, he will quickly master this important ability.

Teach him to squarely face people when speaking and to make brief, but direct, eye contact.

Then begin training your son to make direct and brief eye contact with other people he meets. Some kids are uncomfortable with this type of eye contact, but it is a huge part of the skill of self-confidence!

Voice Projection.

A timid voice is an indication of a lack of self-confidence. Gently coach your child to project his voice.

Teach him that when speaking, he should use deep breathing and speak from deep within his chest (rather than from high in the throat).

He should keep a lot of air in his lungs. Some children also need to slow a little when speaking.

With this posture of confidence:

- Your child will _feel_ empowered. Try these techniques yourself. You immediately feel more confident when assuming these postures. Remember, 54 percent of how we feel comes from what we are doing with our bodies!
- Other people respond to your child with more respect and more care. Bullies leave him alone. Teachers will pay more attention to your son when he looks alert.

When people begin seeing your son as a confident person and treating him accordingly, he will begin to feel like and be a confident person!

Finding and Recalling Victories

Your child's current level of confidence is the sum of all the positive and negative reinforcement she has experienced.

Like all children, she has had both positive and negative experiences. Confident children are in tune with their previous positive experiences. Children without confidence draw their self-images from their negative histories.

Where do you draw your child's attention? Are you quick to remind her of past victories? Or do you keep previous defeats alive? This is how you build confidence—or destroy it!

You need to be a "good-finder," of course. But you also need to be a "good-recaller," too! Often, we dwell on defeats while overlooking or minimizing victories.

Directing, and sometimes redirecting, a child's attention to certain types of memories is an important part of the development of confidence.

Your task is to pile up so many positive experiences in your child's mind that negative experiences don't have a chance.

Your Child's Comfort Zone

Begin to create experiences that move your child outside his comfort zone. *(See illustration.)*

Do you allow your son to retreat into an ever-shrinking comfort zone? Or do you challenge him with new experiences, causing his comfort zone to expand?

It's important that you gently, lovingly, coachingly, consistently, and strategically help him to move outside his current comfort zone.

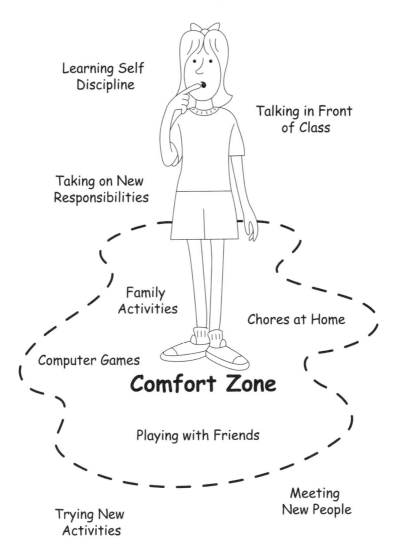

Outside Comfort Zone

Learning Self
Discipline

Talking in Front
of Class

Taking on New
Responsibilities

Family
Activities

Chores at Home

Computer Games

Comfort Zone

Playing with Friends

Meeting
New People

Trying New
Activities

Outside Comfort Zone

It's really not hard. You just need to follow this strategy:

1. A child's lack of confidence will usually manifest itself most clearly in one or two areas. Try to isolate the situations that make your child uncomfortable. Does he get involved in physical activity? Academic pursuits? Social situations?

2. Define what a small step would be. For example, your child might lack confidence in social situations. To develop his confidence, a small step might be to introduce himself to a person he doesn't know very well. If you are focusing on athletics, it might be to take part in a soccer game during recess.

3. Make a plan. Decide what needs to be done. Practice, role-play, and rehearse at home—before your child actually tries to perform these skills in a real situation. Do this as often as it takes for your child to feel comfortable.

4. Execute the plan. Provide all the encouragement and support you can.

5. Review what happened and adjust accordingly. If he gets great results, then move onto the next challenge. If he has a setback, that's okay! Just retrain and start again.

Zeke's Rehearsal of Fear

Zeke was so excited when he received an invitation from his best friend, Jesse, to sleep overnight. He was six years old, and this would be his first time away from home by himself.

He talked about it for days. When the day finally came, Zeke had his gear ready early in the day. However, as they were going out the door, Zeke suddenly developed a stomachache.

"Maybe I better not go," he told his mother. So Mom called Jesse's mom. They rescheduled for the following Friday night.

When the same series of events repeated itself the following Friday, Mom said to herself, "Now I understand. This overnight trip takes Zeke outside his comfort zone!"

So Mom made a plan. She and Zeke rehearsed every part of an overnight trip. They talked about what it would be like to go to sleep in a different house. What would happen at mealtimes. Where he would keep his toothbrush. When Mom would drop him off and pick him up.

So Zeke, with his mother's help, practiced the overnight trip. He even slept in his sleeping bag on the floor of the family room, pretending he was at Jesse's house.

When it came time to try again, Zeke was mildly apprehensive but nothing like before. When it came time to leave, he bravely went out the door. Zeke had a wonderful time and never struggled with this challenge again.

Zeke's mom was smart. She recorded this event in Zeke's "Victory Book" and used it to remind Zeke that he could, in fact, move outside his comfort zone!

Overall Greater Confidence from *One Thing*

Another great way to develop your child's confidence is to help her become an expert in a particular area. Everybody knows that if you are good at something, then you become confident in that thing. Most people don't know, however, that a child's confidence in one area spills over into others.

Many parents have the idea that they want their kids to experience a lot of different things. Even so, being satisfactory at a lot of things does not have the same effect.

It doesn't really matter which area of study you pick. It could be sports, a hobby, martial arts, music, or Scouts. What is important is that you guide your child into an extended commitment to a specific area of study.

Danielle started horseback riding at age eight. She had always been shy, but she loved horses. She took lessons. She learned all about the care and feeding of horses. She rode a lot. She even competed. After a time, she began to earn recognition for her efforts. Even some awards.

It wasn't Danielle's style to brag about her accomplishments. Her friends, however, learned of her skill and respected it.

Mom noticed that Danielle's friends seemed to hold her in high regard. She noticed Danielle being different, too. More of a leader. She was still quiet but was now much more assertive, more sure of herself.

Mom credited Danielle's horseback-riding skill for her increase in confidence.

Remember, being somewhat good at a lot of things does not produce confidence. Being really good at *one* thing does!

Summary.

Consistency is crucial to the development of self-confidence. Your efforts must be ongoing. A big, short-term effort will have little effect.

Always keep in mind that confidence is easier to maintain than it is to restore. It's important to be proactive in this area. Apply these techniques. Reinforce every brave effort. Confidence is one of your child's most prized possessions!

For more tools to build your child's self-esteem, sign up for a free subscription to the Rock Solid Kids Newsletter. Visit www.rocksolidkids.com/newsletter to sign up!

Confidence Exercises

Note: Not all exercises are appropriate for all ages; choose the ones best suited for your child's age and experience level.

Week #1

1. My child has:	☐ Lots of confidence
	☐ Some confidence
	☐ Not much confidence

| 2. An example of my child having self-confidence: |
| |

| 3. An example of my child needing more self-confidence: |
| |

| 4. At the current time, my child's level of self-confidence may be: | ☐ Increasing |
| | ☐ Decreasing |

| 5. Talk with your child about the importance of a confident posture. Look through some magazines or newspapers and cut out some pictures of people who have confident body language. Why does he seem self-confident? How can you tell by looking at his body language that he is self-confident? Help your child tape up a few favorite confident body-language pictures where he will see them each day. |
| ☐ Check here when you have completed this step. |

6. Reread the "Confidence" chapter. List here any additional thoughts, ideas, or action steps that occur to you:

☐ Check here when you have completed all Week #1 Exercises.

Date:

Week #2

1. With your child, practice a confident body-language pose. For example, you might have your child stand with her feet apart, looking toward the sky, punching into the air with one fist while yelling, "Yes!" Rehearse this posture, encouraging your child to do it with passion and enthusiasm. This becomes her "Power Move." Throughout the upcoming week, occasionally say to your child, "Confidence!" Watch as she goes into her new "Power Move."

☐ Check here when you have done this at least five times.

2. Write any thoughts or observations you make regarding the Power Move. Does it seem to affect your child's emotional state? Does it seem to truly empower your child?

3. The "Power Move" can be an important tool in developing your child's self-confidence. Anytime your child is feeling nervous or afraid or has to do something that moves her outside her comfort zone, the "Power Move" will give her Confidence! List five situations where the "Power Move" may be useful.	1. 2. 3. 4. 5.

4. Now let's start your child's "Victory Book." Describe here the type of list you will start. Select the type of format you will use:	☐ Scrapbook ☐ Photo album ☐ Videotape ☐ Other:

5. Now list here some past Victories you will be recording in your child's "Victory Book:"	1. 2. 3. 4. 5.

☐ Check here when you have started your child's "Victory Book" in the format you selected.

Date:

6. Reread the "Confidence" chapter. List here any additional thoughts, ideas, or action steps that occur to you:

☐ Check here when you have completed all Week #2 Exercises.

Date:

Week #3

1. Continue to reinforce your child's "Power Move." Prompt him anytime he needs a Confidence boost.

☐ Check here when you have done at least five "Power-Move" rehearsals.

2. When a person is feeling nervous or afraid, another way to improve his confidence is to use focused eye contact. Sit with your child and have him make eye contact with you. Have him try to hold the eye contact for thirty to sixty seconds without letting go.

☐ Check here when you have done at least five "Eye-Contact" drills.

3. Now let's put the "Eye-Contact" exercise together with the "Power Move." When your child does the "Power Move," make sure he is looking directly at you, eye to eye.

☐ Check here when you have rehearsed the "Power Move" together with "Eye Contact" at least five times over the next week.

4. Show your child the "Victory Book" that you have started. Ask him for ideas about what to include. List some Victories he would like to record here:	1.
	2.
	3.
	4.
	5.

☐ Check here when you have recorded these additional ideas in the Victory List.

5. Reread the "Confidence" chapter. List here any additional thoughts, ideas, or action steps that occur to you:

☐ Check here when you have completed all Week #3 Exercises.

Date:

Week #4

1. Begin making a "Comfort Zone" poster to hang in your child's room. Take a piece of poster board and draw a good-sized circle on it. Inside, list as many things as you can think of that used to be challenging for your child but that she now finds easy to handle. Inside the circle, write: "Comfort Zone" (*see page 81*).

Now outside the circle, list as many things as you can think of that are outside the Comfort Zone. These are things that your child would like to do, or ought to do, but cause a high degree of discomfort for your child.

2. An easy way to develop confidence is to take a challenging task and divide it into small, easy-to-handle steps. Sit with your child and choose two challenges from the Comfort-Zone poster that are outside the Comfort Zone. List them here and break them up into several small steps.	First Challenge
	Mini-Step 1.
	Mini-Step 2.
	Mini-Step 3.
	Mini-Step 4.
	Second Challenge
	Mini-Step 1.
	Mini-Step 2.
	Mini-Step 3.
	Mini-Step 4.

3. Help your child to complete the first two Mini-Steps of each of these challenges. Just starting this exercise will develop confidence!

☐ Check here when she has completed the first two Mini-Steps of each Challenge.

☐ Check here when she has completed the final two Mini-Steps of each Challenge.

4. Continue to reinforce your child's "Power-Move" and "Eye Contact" exercises.

☐ Check here when you have reinforced it at least five times.

☐ Check here when you have completed all Week #4 Exercises.

Date:

5. Another important way to appear and feel confident is to project your voice. If your child has a small, soft voice, then encourage her to put more air in her lungs and speak a little louder, more forcefully (e.g., practice using the word in, say, her "Power Move": **Yes!**").

Remember, the three components of the "Power Move" are body language, eye contact, and voice projection. Over the upcoming weeks, continue to practice and reinforce these important strategies until they become easy and natural for your child!

6. Reread the "Confidence" chapter. List here any additional thoughts, ideas, or action steps that occur to you:

7. Go back and reread the previous chapter, "Respect," the notes you took, and the commitments you made in the exercise segment. List here any thoughts or questions that you have:

8. Nice going, Rock-Solid parents! By completing these exercises, you have already begun to give your child some valuable skills. Take a few minutes right now and review your notes from all previous chapters. Write here three reminders to yourself:

Reminder #1:

Reminder #2:

Reminder #3:

You are now ready to move on to the next chapter!

Your Child's Spiritual Strength: The Four Barriers

To be strong and capable and to handle life's challenges, your child must develop himself spiritually. You may think he's strong in body and agile in mind. However, if he has not developed himself spiritually, he is weak.

As a parent, to teach spirituality, you must have developed spirituality yourself. You must believe you have a spirit. What's more, you must believe, at least in Judeo-Christian terms, that after your body dies, the spirit part of you continues. In other words, your spirit never dies.

For generations, Western philosophy has taught us that we define ourselves using three core realities: mind, body, and spirit. Everybody understands mind and body. They are easy to see: brain, bones, and flesh. On the other hand, since you can't see your spirit, it's harder to understand and accept.

Yet, everything you see—everything that shows itself in *physical* form—once began in *spiritual* form.

In the very first book of the Bible, God said, "Let there be light." A spirit uttered words and created something that revealed itself in physical form. In Judeo-Christian terms, that's how our universe works. The spiritual world is where it begins, with the physical world being an extension of the spiritual.

You (or, more specifically, your body) can feel your spirit. It is the small voice inside you. It rises when you face trials. It lets you know when it's wounded or troubled, when you are less than you should be. It prompts you to be your best.

Ultimately, your spirit is the part of you that knows God (however you define Him)—and prompts you to seek Him.

Like it or not, we are now witnessing a breakdown in Western culture. A spiritual breakdown.

One of the biggest problems facing children today is that they have grown up in a culture that pretty much allows everybody to do as they please.

The Gray Fog between Black and White

Since the 1960s, our society has accepted many types of behavior that were once considered unacceptable: divorce, abortion, cohabitation. For too many of us, we accept them as okay.

It used to be that we had right, and we had wrong. But today, most of us believe that absolutes do not exist, at least when it comes to ideas of right and wrong. Yet, these absolutes, in fact, come with natural, dire consequences. So our kids don't know the price they pay when they choose to disobey these absolutes.

With no absolutes, we end up teaching our kids about a "gray" area between black and white. They are free to define and choose their *own* sense of right and wrong. That may be. Unfortunately, however, they are not free to choose the consequences of their choice. Now you know why God insists that we learn (and obey) the absolutes of correct moral behavior.

To put your children on solid ground, it is vital that you teach them about right and wrong. What's more, that it's not all that difficult to see which is which.

Even so, your child may fight several battles while she's developing morally and spiritually.

Battle #1.

Some people believe that spiritual things are signs of weakness. They believe they can be "self-reliant" or successful on their own, without God. How foolish!

When I was a kid, many of my friends had the idea that being spiritual was a sign of weakness and that it was for sissies. Or just that it somehow wasn't cool.

I urge you to teach your kids that a strong spirit, in fact, is a sign of strength. With our sons, Jason and Ian, I taught them about the heroes of the Bible. I showed them that courageous men and women paid attention to their spiritual health, allowing them to do powerful deeds.

Battle #2.

I hear some parents say that they are *not* going to impose their spiritual beliefs on their children: "We're just going to let them make up their own mind when they're older!"

How sad. How many of us decide we are not going to teach our children about, say, our beliefs about finances or about family relationships? Or that we are not going to expose them to our beliefs about good health habits?

So ask yourself, should you impose your beliefs on your kids? *Of course!* You must teach them to stand for something—to believe in something.

Battle #3.

Your children will learn the wrong lesson if you insist on waiting. Worse, you may find it's too late if it takes hitting the bottom of the barrel before seeking spiritual guidance.

On the other hand, if you've totally exhausted your personal resources and are at the end of your rope (and out of sheer desperation, you turn to God), will He bail you out? Probably.

However, is it better to proactively seek Him—to develop a relationship with Him *before* you are in hot water? Of course. With your proactive example, will your children be better prepared to face *their* life's journey? Absolutely!

Battle #4.

Maybe you are not clear on what you believe. That's okay. It's not too late. If you haven't yet clarified and developed your own spiritual beliefs, why not approach God? He will welcome you into His presence.

Or maybe you used to be close to God but have slipped away. That's okay, too. God is constant and wants to have a relationship with you. Approach Him. Say, "I've been away for a while, Lord. But I'd like to return."

He is faithful and true.

It's not too late, no matter how old you are. So take some action steps. Sit down with that Bible or visit that church or synagogue. Or talk to friends who are involved in spiritual pursuits. Your children will respect and thank you for it.

More than this, your children will learn how to go about exploring their own beliefs. Your example will give them the faith to embark on that ultimate of spiritual journeys: that someone is, in fact, listening.

Summary.

My belief is that a loving and just God made us in His own likeness. Whatever your particular faith, to have a strong spirit you must have this same key belief, that God created you in His image. If you believe that your spirit is eternal, then you must recognize that someday you will be going back to where you came—back to Him!

Unless you believe in something greater than yourself—something eternal—I don't think it really matters what you do. If you believe you descended from monkeys, if you believe that God is a fairy tale, that no one will ultimately judge your actions, then who cares what you do? Those ideas can only lead you to believe that everything just boils down to what you can get away with.

On the other hand, if you believe you are here because of God, then you must also believe that you are accountable to Him. If that's true, then you, both as an individual and as a parent, are under an obligation to seek the mind of God. You need to find out what He expects of you, especially when it comes to raising your children. Once you do, be assured that He won't be shy about telling you what he expects.

Spiritual Development Exercises
Note: Not all exercises are appropriate for all ages; choose the ones best suited for your child's age and experience level.

Week #1

1. My child has a:	☐ Strong level of Spiritual Development
	☐ Moderate level of Spiritual Development
	☐ Low level of Spiritual Development

2. Our family has a:	☐ Strong level of Spiritual Development
	☐ Moderate level of Spiritual Development
	☐ Low level of Spiritual Development

3. Write a brief description of your personal Spiritual beliefs:

4. Now list some of your family's Spiritual Development activities (e.g., church/ synagogue attendance, family prayer, Bible study, etc.):	1.
	2.
	3.
	4.
	5.

5. Reread the "Spiritual Development" chapter. List here any additional thoughts, ideas, or action steps that occur to you:

☐ Check here when you have completed all Week #1 Exercises.

Date:

Week #2

1. Describe your Spiritual heritage. What type of beliefs or Spiritual activities did you grow up with?

```
┌──────────────────────────────────────────────┐
│                                                │
│                                                │
│                                                │
│                                                │
│                                                │
└──────────────────────────────────────────────┘
```

2. Have any of your beliefs changed since then? If so, how?

3. Visit a bookstore and browse through the Spiritual Development section. Pick up a book that is consistent with your particular faith or belief system.

☐ Check here when you have completed your four sessions.

4. Reread the "Spiritual Development" chapter. List here any additional thoughts, ideas, or action steps that occur to you:

☐ Check here when you have completed all Week #2 Exercises.

Date:

Week #3

1. If our family were spiritually strong, what would we be doing?	1.
	2.
	3.

	4.
	5.

2. The two steps I commit to for my family are …	1.
(Commit to two of the steps identified in Step 1. Choose two that you can begin right away.)	2.

| 3. List any obstacles you might encounter in carrying out the two action steps you have chosen: | Obstacle 1. |
| | Obstacle 2. |

4. I will handle Obstacle 1 by …

5. I will handle Obstacle 2 by …

☐ Check here if you are continuing to read the book you started last week and have completed four fifteen-minute sessions.

6. Reread the "Spiritual Development" chapter. List here any additional thoughts, ideas, or action steps that occur to you:

☐ Check here when you have completed all Week #3 Exercises.

Date:

Week #4

☐ Check here when you have completed the two action steps you committed to last week.

1. Describe the experience of completing Step 1:

2. Describe the experience of completing Step 2:

☐ Check here when you have completed all Week #4 Exercises.

☐ Check here if you are continuing to read the book you started last week and have done four fifteen-minute sessions.

3. Describe here the ongoing "Spiritual Development" activities you plan to pursue. Describe everything you would do in a week:	1.
	2.
	3.
	4.
	5.

4. Now list any other monthly, annual, or other type of activities you commit to:	1.
	2.
	3.

| 5. Reread the "Spiritual Development" chapter. List here any additional thoughts, ideas, or action steps that occur to you: |
| |

☐ Check here when you have completed all Week #4 Exercises.

Date:

6. Go back and reread the previous chapter, "Confidence," the notes you took, and the commitments you made in the Exercise segment. List here any thoughts, progress, or questions:

Well done, "Rock-Solid" parents! A strong emphasis on Spiritual Development is one of the most powerful ways to raise a happy, healthy, confident child. Take a moment, give yourself a pat on the back, and let's move on.

Get a FREE subscription to Keith Hafner's Rock Solid Kids newsletter at www.rocksolidkids.com/newsletter!

A Window on Your Child's Self-Image

How simple our world would be if everyone were honest. Consider for a minute how much of our lives are dedicated to protecting ourselves from the dishonesty of others.

It is significant that one of our country's oldest stories involves the honesty of our first president, George Washington. He chopped down the cherry tree. His father asked him about it, and he said, "I cannot tell a lie. I did it." At the foundation of this quaint little story is the quality of honesty. It's no wonder this story has survived for decades.

Honesty is more than simply avoiding lies. It includes a belief in and a pursuit of the truth.

To develop a positive self-image, to have healthy relationships with other people, honesty must be present.

Honesty is a sure sign of healthy self-esteem. Why? Because an honest person takes responsibility for her actions. She feels good about herself and has no need to resort to deception.

Dishonesty comes with several problems:

1. A dishonest person loses the trust of other people. When you catch someone lying to you, trust breaks down. From that day on, you question everything that person says.

2. A dishonest person has trouble trusting others. She knows of her own dishonesty, so she assumes that others are dishonest.

3. Without honesty, people lose touch with reality. If a person tells a lie often enough, she will begin to believe it.

4. When a person begins to be dishonest, her behavior quickly worsens. She believes that since she isn't going to tell the truth anyway, she might as well do whatever she pleases.

How to Teach Honesty

Dishonesty is learned behavior. A child will learn to lie if it "makes sense" to lie. For example, if:

- He senses that telling the truth will lead to a loss of love or approval.
- He observes you lying.
- You accidentally teach him to lie by penalizing him for telling the truth.

To avoid these and other problems, you must teach honesty using the following tools:

1. *Unconditional Love.* You can unwittingly teach a child to be dishonest. You allow your child to feel that your love for him is conditional love. Kids will lie if they think that the truth will cause a lack of love or approval.

If your love for your child is performance based—or if he *believes* it is performance based—you've created a situation where it really makes sense for your child to lie!

Make sure you teach your children that you love them no matter what, *unconditionally!* That no matter what happens, or what kinds of actions they may take, there is nothing that would interfere with your love and your support for them. No matter what, you will always be there for them.

2. *Your Example.* Maybe more than any of the "Rock-Solid" skills, your example teaches honesty. On the other hand, your child will learn to be dishonest if he observes even the slightest hesitation in your commitment to honesty.

For example:

- The phone rings. It's your neighbor calling. You can't talk. You tell your son, "Tell her I'm not home!"
- In the movie line, you say to your twelve-year-old, "Remember, you're only eleven."
- You are leaving the grocery store. You say, "It's our lucky day. They didn't charge us for some of the things we bought!"

3. *Emotional Honesty.* It's also important that you teach your child to be honest with himself, especially with emotions.

Consider this: Margaret is playing quite contentedly by herself in the living room. Along comes Greg, age four, asking questions and being a mild nuisance. Margaret has no patience for Greg's questions. Unexpectedly, she explodes! She yells at him, saying that he's stupid and to get away from her. She provokes quite a scene, and poor Greg runs crying to Mom.

Well, Margaret may be annoyed with Greg—on the surface. But then you start talking to her about what she's feeling. Some careful questions reveal that something happened at school today that was upsetting to her.

Margaret found out that her best friend, Shannon, was having a sleepover and that she had failed to invite her. She has been upset all day, provoking her to lash out at her brother. Margaret would not have quarreled with Greg if she had been honest about how she felt at school. Greg would have made out better, too.

Unless Margaret learns to be honest emotionally, she will continue to experience these types of frustrations without understanding why.

When it comes to their emotions, we can help our kids develop a more thorough level of honesty. We can help them see the connections.

Here's what Margaret's mother could have done to defuse this situation:

Mom: "You don't usually snap at Greg, Margaret. Is everything okay?"

Margaret: "Yeah, I'm okay, I guess."

Mom: "How did it go at school today? Anything happen?"

Margaret: "No, not really."

Mom: "What's up with your friends lately?"

Margaret: "I don't know—but that Shannon, I hate her!"

It takes some persistence to uncover these types of emotions.

You see that Margaret had covered up her true feelings. Mom had to probe three questions deep before Margaret revealed what was really bothering her. She probably wasn't trying to be evasive. She may not have been aware that she was so upset with her friend.

It takes a long time before your kids have the maturity to sort these things out on their own. Just look around at all the adults who struggle with this type of thing!

Important Note: "Rock-Solid" parents will want to keep in mind that if a child does something wrong and lies about it, the lie is often the bigger of the two infractions.

Joseph swipes a cookie from the jar.

Dad asks, "Joseph, did you take a cookie without permission?"

"No!" replies Joseph with cookie crumbs all over his face.

Swiping a cookie is a small infraction. The lie isn't. It says, "I will cover my actions with lies to protect myself."

When your child does something wrong and lies, two offenses have been committed. You need to treat them as two!

Marshall, ten, knew that it was a clear violation of the rules the day he rode his bike to the mall. Marshall's next-door neighbor saw Marshall and thought it strange that he was so far from home. She was concerned that Marshall was doing something he shouldn't have been doing, so she called Marshall's mom and let her know.

Marshall's mom confronted him. Marshall took a deep breath and admitted to the rule violation.

His mom thought about what to do. She was unhappy about the rule violation but happy that Marshall had told the truth.

If Marshall had lied, then his mom would have said, "One week of grounding for the rule violation and another week for lying." But since he had been truthful, he received only one punishment.

Later that week, his mom continued to reinforce Marshall's truthfulness. She said to Marshall, "Honey, I was so proud of the way that you told the truth about going to the mall. I respect you for that."

If Mom had failed to acknowledge and appreciate Marshall's honesty, she might have accidentally taught him to lie. If your child sees no payoff from telling the truth, he might begin to think, "Maybe I should have lied. I mean, look at all the trouble I got into for telling the truth."

Reinforce your child's honesty whenever you can. Use statements like these:

- "I respect your honesty!"
- "I like the way you take pride in being truthful."
- "I trust you because of your honesty."

Remember that telling the truth does not allow your child to escape the consequences of his actions. Your appreciation of his honesty is separate.

Immediate Honesty

Telling the truth means telling it immediately. If a child lies first, then tells the truth when the lie fails, it's not the same. Insist on immediate honesty.

President Clinton set a dangerous precedent for our children. He lied for months about his involvement with Monica Lewinsky. He told the truth only when it became absolutely necessary. Some of his supporters said, "We are so proud of the President for making this difficult decision to tell the truth."

Why should he have to "decide" to tell the truth? It was not really telling the truth when he finally came clean after months of lying and after the truth was already evident.

Honesty Exercises

Note: Not all exercises are appropriate for all ages; choose the ones best suited for your child's age and experience level.

Week #1

1. My child is:	☐ Always honest
	☐ Usually honest
	☐ Having a problem with honesty

2. Give an example of honesty on your child's part:

3. Give an example of your child being less than honest:

4. List any ways that you might have unintentionally taught your child to be dishonest. (You might want to look at the text in the "Honesty" chapter to review how dishonesty is unintentionally taught.)	1.
	2.
	3.

5. Reread the "Honesty" chapter. List here any additional thoughts, ideas, or action steps that occur to you:

☐ Check here when you have completed all Week #1 Exercises.

Date:

Week #2

1. Last week, we listed any ways that you might be unintentionally teaching your child to be dishonest. If you uncovered any ways, list here how you will handle those situations differently in the future:	1. Before, I did this:
	In the future, I will do this:
	2. Before, I did this:
	In the future, I will do this:
	3. Before, I did this:
	In the future, I will do this:

2. Does my child cover up her true feelings? If so, list some examples here:

3. Some children have a problem with honesty because they fear that if they are honest, they will lose their parents' love. Here are some things you can say that will assure your child that your love is unconditional. Put a check beside the ones you plan to use.	☐ "I will always love you, no matter what!" ☐ "You can tell me anything!" ☐ "No need for secrets between you and me!" ☐ Other:

4. Use at least one of these affirmations when talking with your child. Describe here the situation and how your child responded. Also, how did you feel?

5. Reread the "Honesty" chapter. List here any additional thoughts, ideas, or action steps that occur to you:

☐ Check here when you have completed all Week #2 Exercises.

Date:

Week #3

1. If my child breaks a rule, is he honest about what he has done? Or does he try to cover his actions with dishonesty? List a couple examples of honest or dishonest behavior here:

2. Reread the part in the "Honesty" chapter that discusses separating the rule violation for the honesty. List here any observations you have:

3. When my child breaks a rule, I understand the importance of separating the action from the truth telling. If my child breaks a rule and is honest about his actions, here's how I will handle it:

If he breaks a rule and lies about it, then here's how I will handle it:

4. With your child, find some examples of people being either honest or dishonest. What were the consequences of their actions? For example, a child who has told a lie might lose the trust of his parents. List some honest or dishonest actions and their consequences here:

ACTION:

CONSEQUENCE:

ACTION:

CONSEQUENCE:

5. Reread the "Honesty" chapter. List here any additional thoughts, ideas, or action steps that occur to you:

☐ Check here when you have completed all Week #3 Exercises.
Date:

Week #4

1. Think about your commitment to express unconditional love for your child. Reread the exercises from Week #2 that deal with unconditional love. Why is it important that your child understands that your love is unconditional? List some reasons here:	1. 2. 3.

2. Discuss some situations with your child where choosing to be honest might be hard. How would you handle the following?	1. The cashier gives you the wrong change, accidentally overpaying you. What do you do?
	2. Somebody calls you on the phone. You don't want to talk to her. How do you handle it?
	3. Other (Think of an example that will be about your child and write it down here; how will you handle it?)

3. Reread the "Honesty" chapter. List here any additional thoughts, ideas, or action steps that occur to you:

☐ Check here when you have completed all Week #4 Exercises.

Date:

4. Go back and reread the previous chapter, "Spiritual Development," the notes you took, and the commitments you made in the Exercise segment. List here any thoughts, progress, or questions that you have:

Great job! By now, you may already be seeing new and exciting things from your child. Let's stay focused. Continue to work on one chapter each month. Try to reinforce the skills covered in the previous month's work. You have already improved your child's potential to be Happy, Healthy, and Confident! You are ready to move on to the next chapter!

Keep yourself focused on building a Rock Solid Kid - sign up for the FREE Rock Solid Kids Newsletter at www.rocksolidkids.com/newsletter.

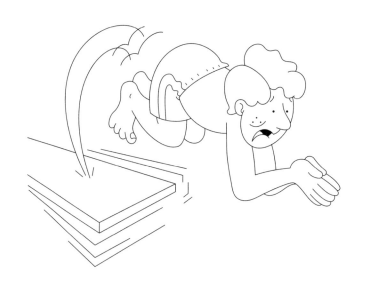

Going for It, Even When You're Scared Stiff

Courage is probably the most interesting of the "Rock-Solid" skills. Courage fascinates both kids and adults. We love adventure stories. We love super heroes. Tales of courage have been handed down from generation to generation.

Not only is courage interesting. In a difficult, unsympathetic world, courage is essential.

Courage is essential because people will always appear to attack the good; they'll challenge all points of view based on the absolutes of correct moral behavior. By extension, they will also test a person's courage—including your child's.

Courage is also one of the most misunderstood of the "Rock-Solid" skills. Many people think that courage shows a lack of fear. Not true!

Courage doesn't mean we are not afraid. It means we can *function effectively* despite our fear. People who appear courageous have the same feelings of fear that you and I experience.

However, courageous people understand that scary people, obstacles, and circumstances melt away when they are confronted with courage.

A *lack* of courage eventually leads to low self-esteem. If a person is constantly afraid, he feels less and less able to deal with his surroundings. Instead of experiencing growth, he shrinks. He moves from situation to situation inside an ever-shrinking comfort zone.

The most important reason for your child to develop courage is that it determines how much freedom he will experience. Fear will hold your child back. It will prevent him from trying new things, from pursuing meaningful opportunities, and from living the life he was meant to live.

- Peter used to love playing in the neighborhood playground. But since he had an encounter with some older kids, he refuses to go. The older kids didn't harm him, but their aggressive way of playing and speaking has intimidated Peter. Even though he would rather be on the playground, he now sits in the house watching television.

- Curtis always followed the rules. As he entered junior high school, however, some kids began to make friends with him. Unfortunately, these were kids who didn't have the same commitment to following the rules. Succumbing to peer pressure, Curtis began to miss curfews and go to places that were off limits. Additionally, his grades began to drop. Curtis lacked the courage to resist negative peer pressure.

- Courtney wants to be a veterinarian. However, she has always heard that the ACT, the college entrance exam, is difficult. Even though she has always been a good student, she has postponed signing up for the test. Will her lack of courage prevent her from pursuing her dream?

These children have allowed fear to restrict their freedom. With some appropriate instruction in courage, they can conquer these fears and do the things they should be doing!

How to Teach Courage

One of the best ways to develop courage is to simply decide that you will have courage and commit to it. Each of us, in our own lives, faces an important decision:

"How will I handle the tough challenges that come my way? Will I confront life's obstacles head on? Or will I shrink from scary situations? Will I retreat to a place where it always feels safe?"

Courage is a decision you make. You decide to have courage. With young children, however, you must decide for them. You must decide:

- "Will my child live a courageous, empowered life?"
- "Am I committed to helping her develop these skills?"

If you wait until your child is old enough to understand these things by herself, it will be too late!

You must make these decisions about courage in advance. You cannot wait until scary circumstances force you to behave courageously. In the same way, you can't wait until your child is frightened about something to begin this process.

After deciding to live a courageous life, the next step is to understand the body language of courage.

Can you picture how a courageous person looks? How she would be standing? Her posture, her voice; the way she would look you in the eye? Of course you can.

This is why we love Batman, John Wayne, and Mighty Mouse. Not only are they courageous, but they also look courageous! We can see the courage in their body language!

Fear, too, has its own body language. Can you picture how a "scaredy-cat" would look? Sure you can.

When confronted with a scary situation, the body has a reaction: "This has happened before!" The goose bumps, sweaty palms, rapid pulse, and shallow breathing. The shaky knees, the chill that runs down your spine, and the feeling that you can't move. You panic! Not because of what is going on externally but because of what's happening to your body.

When Jason, my older son, was about five years old, he participated in his first martial arts demonstration. He was a beginning martial art student at the time. Jason had a major part in a skit that we were doing. At the end of the skit, he had to run out onto the stage. He then kicked all the "bad guys," knocking them down, until he was the only one left standing. He was there on the stage all by himself—everybody else was on the ground. Of course, the audience cheered and clapped. Then the performers stood up and ran off the stage.

As we prepared to leave, I felt Jason tapping on my leg from behind. "Dad! Dad! Something's wrong. I don't know what it is."

I said, "What's the matter?"

He said, "Right here in my chest—it keeps going boom, boom, boom, and it won't stop."

His role so pumped and excited him, his heart was pounding. It was the first time that had happened to him, and he didn't know what it was!

This fear response happens to all of us. To develop courage, you must understand how to replace the panic feeling with a feeling of calmness and control.

You must follow three important steps to remain calm and in control:

1. Get your breathing under control. Take slow, deep breaths, breathing deeply into the bottom of your lungs.
2. Maintain your physical balance. Distribute your weight evenly and shift to the balls of your feet.
3. Relax your muscles, especially your face, shoulders, and hands.

Chloe's mom, Mrs. Simmons, taught her daughter to remember breathing, balance, and relaxing. She would say, "Okay, Chloe, something happens, and you become scared. What do you do?"

Chloe said, "Breathing, Balance, and Relaxing."

Mom said, "That's good! Show me what it looks like."

Chloe took three deep breaths and said, "Breathing!" She distributed her weight evenly and said, "Balance!" Simultaneously, she relaxed her face, shoulders, and hands and said, "Relaxing!"

If Chloe continues to repeat this exercise, then her courage will increase, allowing her to control her fear!

So remember: Control the physical response, and your child will always have the courage she needs!

Also never forget that your child has a "comfort zone." The farther your child moves from the center of her comfort zone, the more she will experience fear. Therefore, her need for courage will increase.

So the next step in developing courage is to simply expand the size of your child's "comfort zone."

You can do this by challenging that comfort zone's boundaries. Smart "Rock-Solid" parents gently and lovingly guide their children with practiced risk-taking. They gradually challenge the boundaries of the comfort zone. This is a process—not an event.

To move your child outside her comfort zone, you must give support by being there and offering your encouragement. It's a lot like teaching a child to ride a two-wheel bike. You must walk beside her, supporting the bike, giving verbal encouragement. If you let go too early, then she crashes. If you hang on too long, then she never learns to ride alone.

Many children never learn courage because Mom and Dad don't spend sufficient time "walking beside the bike."

Max, age eight, began going to the city pool. Many of his friends went, too. They enjoyed jumping into the deep end and did it seemingly without fear. Even though Max could swim, he was terrified of deep water. He began saying that he didn't want to go to the pool. Max's dad understood that Max needed some help in conquering his fear. He began taking Max to the pool early Saturday mornings.

Dad would hold Max's hand while Max jumped. Dad would hang on and pull Max out. Even this safe step took a lot of courage for Max. After Max was comfortable with this system, Dad began getting into the water, and Max would jump into his dad's outstretched arms. Then Dad and Max would jump into the water together.

After several Saturday morning sessions, something clicked in Max. He could jump into the deep end all by himself, without any fear whatsoever.

Max's dad did the right thing. He knew that breaking a scary task into a series of small steps could reduce fear to a level his child could better manage. So remember, the comfort zone often expands in small steps, not by big leaps.

Sounds like a lot of work, doesn't it? But I've got a question for you. How much work do you think it is to have a kid who is frequently afraid?

It's not really as much work as you might think to develop courage. This approach develops reserves of courage. After conquering one fear, it makes the next one easier. After your child has conquered several, she's empowered to do just about anything!

Another powerful tool in developing courage is visualization. When you imagine something happening, a mental image appears in your mind. It's almost like watching a movie. Think about a scary situation. You run this situation like a movie in your head, and you end up feeling scared.

But guess what? You can change the movie anyway you want! When you change the visual picture, you change the emotion it produces.

Matt's fourth grade teacher, Mrs. Taylor, required each child to read a report in front of the class. Matt was terrified! The thought of being in front of the class filled him with fear. He was running mental movies in which he failed horribly.

Matt's mother understood the power of visualization. She knew that Matt was already running a movie in his head—a movie with a bad outcome. Matt needed her help to change the movie to one with a positive outcome.

She had Matt sit with his eyes closed and then said: "Matt, it's your turn to go to the front of the classroom and talk to the class. You feel so calm. Your muscles are loose. You're breathing easily. You move without hurrying. You actually enjoy your time in front of the class. You finish your presentation, and everybody applauds. You have a huge smile on your face as you return to your seat. You feel great!"

As she spoke, Matt would be imagining himself handling the assignment successfully.

Mom repeated this process for Matt, creating vivid pictures. Each time she repeated the procedure, it strengthened his new visual image, forcing the old, scary image to fade away.

Mom's next task is to teach Matt to replay this mental image on his own. He can call upon the same positive visual images whenever the scary pictures return.

Of course, visualization works best if you prepare ahead of time, before your child actually becomes afraid.

If you are skeptical about this working, just remember that your child is using this visualization system already. But, she is using it to make herself afraid!

No Harm Shall Befall You

Finally, faith and trust in God will provide more courage and more feeling of well-being than anything else you can do.

When you have faith that you are under His protection, you know that no real harm can come to you! In Psalm 91, the Lord says, "If you make the Most High your dwelling … then no harm shall befall you."

God's promises have given me courage more times than I can count. When my sons were very young, I began to teach them to stand on God's promises, too. You can do the same.

Summary.

It requires parents who have courage to raise a courageous child. Watching your child move outside the comfort zone can be difficult. You may find yourself retreating into your comfort zone to avoid the uncomfortable experience.

Commit yourself to encouraging your child in anyway you can. Don't allow him to become discouraged. You have tremendous influence over whether your child gains or loses courage!

Courage Exercises
Note: Not all exercises are appropriate for all ages; choose the ones best suited for your child's age and experience level.

Week #1

1. My child has:	☐ A lot of courage
	☐ Some courage
	☐ Not much courage

2. Describe a situation where your child has been Courageous:

3. Now describe a situation where your child could have used more Courage:

4. List some situations, in the future, where your child will need to be Courageous:

5. Reread the "Courage" chapter. List here any additional thoughts, ideas, or action steps that occur to you:

☐ Check here when you have completed all Week #1 Exercises.

Date:

Week #2

1. Last week, we listed future situations where your child will need to be Courageous. Choose one future situation particularly important to your child and write it here:

2. Now break that situation into as many small steps as possible. For example, if you have chosen "Beginning School" as your exercise, you might list small steps like: talking about school, visiting the school, reading a book about a child going to school, or meeting the teacher. List as many steps as possible:	1. 2. 3. 4. 5. 6. 7.

3. Sit down with your child and say, "When you are scared, you need to make sure that you are relaxed and breathing deeply." Then rehearse these skills with your child, as described in the "Courage" chapter. Explain to your child that you will prompt her with the words, "Breathing, Balance, Relaxing" when you see her becoming nervous or frightened. Practice this procedure several times this week.

☐ Check here when you have practiced this on at least six occasions.

4. Reread the "Courage" chapter. List here any additional thoughts, ideas, or action steps that occur to you:

☐ Check here when you have completed all Week #2 Exercises.

Date:

Week #3

1. Last week, we took a potentially scary activity and broke it up into small steps. Do at least three of those steps. Describe here what happened:

2. Continue to work on the "Breathing, Balance, Relaxing" procedure. Explain to your child that he can use this procedure without your help. Say something like, "Okay, you are getting a little nervous. What do you say?" "Breathing, Relax, Mom!" "And what do you do?" "I relax my muscles and take three deep breaths!" "Yes, good job, Marcus!"

☐ Check here when you have rehearsed the "Breathing, Balance, Relaxing" procedure six more times.

3. Discuss the "Comfort Zone" with your child. Remind him that there are things he can easily do now even though they used to be scary. With your child, list things that used to be scary but are now comfortable:	1. 2. 3. 4. 5.
4. Now list some things that are still scary but can be moved inside the comfort zone with a little effort:	1. 2. 3. 4. 5.
5. It is important that your child has a "Statement of Courage." Select one from the following list or create your own.	☐ "I can do scary things!" ☐ "I decide to live a courageous life!" ☐ "I am a courageous, confident person!" ☐ (write your own) _____

Rehearse the chosen "Statement of Courage." Create a little drill with your child, something like this:

Dad: "What type of person are you, Elizabeth?"

Elizabeth: "I am a courageous, confident person, Dad!"

Next write that statement down on a card and tape it in a prominent place in your child's room: on the door or over the bed.

Continue to rehearse the "Statement of Courage" at every opportunity. Coach your child to say this statement on her own, whenever she feels herself moving outside of her comfort zone.

---

6. Reread the "Courage" chapter. List here any additional thoughts, ideas, or action steps that occur to you:

☐ Check here when you have completed all Week #3 Exercises.

Date:

Week #4

1. In week #2, we took a potentially scary activity and broke it into small steps. Do at least three more of those steps. Describe here what happened:

2. Continue to work on both the "Breathing, Balance, Relaxing" procedure and the "Statement of Courage." When you have practiced each procedure at least six times, check the box.	☐ "Breathing, Balance, Relaxing" procedure ☐ "Statement of Courage"
3. Last week, we made a list of things that were outside your child's comfort zone. List a few more things that are currently outside the comfort zone but that you would like to bring into the comfort zone:	1. 2. 3. 4. 5.
4. Earlier we took an activity that required courage on the part of your child and broke it into small steps. List some other activities that can be handled the same way:	1. 2. 3. 4. 5.

It will be easy to work on these activities in the same way we handled the earlier activity. Circle the numbers of the two activities that you plan to tackle next.

☐ Check here when you have completed all Week #4 Exercises.

Date:

5. Go back and reread the previous chapter, "Honesty," the notes you took, and the commitments you made in the Exercise segment. List here any thoughts or questions that you have:

Well done! You have already improved your child's potential to be happy, healthy, and confident! You are ready to move on to the next chapter.

Positive reinforcement is an important part of teaching courage to your child. Receive a FREE report titled "100 Ways to Say 'Great Job!'" at www.rocksolidkids.com/reports/.

Foundation Stone Nine: Contribution

If Your Child Wants More, Then Teach Him to *Give* More

Life isn't fair!

"Why does Marcus get 'A's', and I get 'C's?'"

"Why is Stephanie an athlete, and I'm just a couch potato?"

"Why is Ryan popular, and I'm always lonely?"

If you've ever found your child expressing views similar to these, he's missed one of life's fundamental realities:

Life rewards you in direct proportion to your ability to contribute.

The quality and the quantity of your contribution determine the rewards you will receive. Life not only rewards you in proportion, but it also rewards you in kind.

If you make a valuable contribution, life will reward you with things of value.

If you contribute love, life will reward you with love.

Contribute respect, and life will reward you with respect.

Contribute trouble, and life will reward you with trouble.

Lots of people don't understand why they are getting the results they are getting. They never seem to realize that their results are the right results. They represent the sum of all their contributions … both in quantity and quality.

When you grasp this idea, success becomes simple: contribute more, and you will receive more.

As smart parents, we must teach our kids to contribute:
- Generously of their time, money, and possessions.
- Effort, ideas, enthusiasm, and hustle.
- And find things that need improvement and improve them.

Belief in Abundance

The world is a place of abundance. God created everything we needed and put it here for us to use. Yet many people believe in scarcity, that there's only so much to go around.

Their beliefs are wrong, but they'll get what they believe.

The "scarcity" mentality makes it very hard for you to be a good contributor. Your core belief is that the world does not have unlimited resources. Anytime I gain, you lose. It's every man for himself.

God did not mean for us to live in a self-serving, greedy way. He created an abundant life for us to enjoy and share with others.

Consider the tiny acorn. Plant it and watch it grow. You can build a house with its miraculous powers. It comes with the seeds of its own replacement, multiplied 100,000 times.

The acorn isn't unique. It represents the abundant nature of the universe! Some "acorns" take the form of ideas that you can plant, raise, and harvest. Others take the form of opportunities that you can develop and profit from.

Most of us never come close to tapping into the abundance freely available to us. To avoid this problem, always remember that contribution is the natural result of a belief in abundance.

Give First

Teach your child that there is enough for everybody. Enough time, love, opportunity, and resource. This important belief will make it easy for her to be a person who contributes.

Life rewards you in direct proportion to your ability to contribute. It also requires that you contribute first.

You must plant the seed before you can harvest the crop.

A contributor doesn't mind giving effort, time, or money without immediate reward. Like the smart farmer, she understands that she is planting seeds that will produce fruit in the future.

Some people never begin to plant because they expect immediate rewards. How foolish! Imagine a farmer who failed to plant, insisting that the harvest come immediately.

When a person experiences good fortune, it is the result of seeds already planted.

Miles and Nicholas lived next door to each other. They played ball or rode bikes together nearly every day. In some ways, they were similar to each other. In others, they were different.

Miles always seemed to turn up when somebody in the neighborhood needed help. If a neighbor needed her groceries carried in or some yard work done, more often than not, Miles was there, lending a hand. When neighbors needed somebody to look after a pet or water the plants when they were on vacation, everybody knew that they could rely on Miles.

Nicholas was different. When people needed help, he made himself scarce. He couldn't understand why Miles was always putting out to serve others. "Why are you always doing things for all these people? You never even get paid!"

Miles would shrug and say, "I just like to help out, I guess."

Nicholas considered Miles foolish for doing so much extra work. Yet, he also noticed that Miles also received a lot of "good breaks."

If a family had an extra ticket to a ball game, it was Miles they usually thought of.

He was a regular guest at neighborhood barbeques and pool parties.

Many neighborhood families remembered Miles with a gift at Christmastime.

Meanwhile, Nicholas saw no connection between Miles' contributing attitude and the many invitations and gifts he received. He would often complain to Miles, "Why does everybody like you better than me?"

In late spring, Mrs. Garvey was holding her annual garage sale. Mrs. Garvey had lived in the neighborhood for over forty years, and her garage sale was a huge neighborhood event. When Nicholas and Miles saw the cars parked along the street, they rode by on their bikes to check things out.

Passing by the clothes, the books, and the tools, their attention was quickly drawn to the nearly new mountain bike prominently displayed.

"That used to be my grandson's bike, but he got a new one. You boys in the market for a new bike?" Mrs. Garvey said.

That bright red mountain bike was about the coolest thing that either boy had ever seen. Their spirits fell quickly, though, when they saw Mrs. Garvey's handwritten price tag: $200.

"I wish!" Nicholas said, as the boys waved and rode away.

As the weekend progressed, both boys found themselves riding by Mrs. Garvey's house to look at the bike. Although it was way out of reach, they just had to see if anybody had claimed the awesome prize.

Mrs. Garvey saw the boys admiring the bike. When she happened to see Miles ride by alone, she waved him over. "You like this bike a lot, don't you, Miles?"

"Yes, ma'am. You bet!"

Mrs. Garvey had noticed the worn-out condition of Miles' bike. She had noticed other things, too. Like the way Miles always seemed to appear when somebody needed a hand.

He was good with the younger children in the neighborhood, too. All the kids looked up to Miles. Mrs. Garvey knew that Miles never failed to set a good example.

She also knew that when her friend Mrs. Calvitt got sick, Miles had stopped by every day. He wanted to see if he could do anything to help or bring anything to her.

"I've noticed, young man, the fine job you do around this neighborhood."

Miles felt a little uncomfortable. After all, his parents raised him to believe that helping others was his responsibility.

"Well, I'm making you a gift of this bike. I won't take 'No' for an answer. I just want to thank you for being such a wonderful friend."

You'd think that riding two bikes home at the same time would be hard. Not the way Miles felt. When he showed the bike to his dad, his dad said, "Miles, I've seen how you handle your responsibilities in our neighborhood. You've earned this bike. I'm proud of you."

When Nicholas heard about Miles' good fortune, it astonished him. He complained to his mother, "Why does Miles get all the breaks?"

Mom said, "Well, you know, Miles does a lot for the people in this neighborhood."

Nicholas replied, "I'd do things for people, too, if they were always giving me cool stuff."

I wish this ended with Nicholas observing and learning from his friend, but, sadly, he didn't. Like many of us, he never got it. He always felt that he would begin contributing when good breaks started coming his way.

Miles asked for nothing. He expected nothing in return. But invitations, gifts, and all the rewards that come to contributors came easily to him—because Miles gave first.

Besides contributing first, it's also important to teach our children to contribute more.

Rise Above the Crowd

Some people say, "I'd do more if they paid me more." Or, "I'd be nicer if my spouse was nicer."

A simple truth ensures success in any situation: "Do *more* than people expect of you."

- If your coach expects five laps, do six.
- If your teacher assigns ten problems, do twelve.
- If you are supposed to sell twenty-five per day, sell thirty.

Life becomes easy when you do more than people expect. Do more, and you rise above the crowd.

On the other hand, many people have made a science of doing as little as possible.

This tight-fisted attitude robs everybody, especially the person who has it! This was what Carly's mother had reminded her about before Carly began her part-time summer job. Of course, for Carly, this was merely a review. Her mother had taught her this key principle since she was a child.

Her job was at The Gap, a huge clothing store that catered to high school and college kids. The store carried jeans, sweaters, and anything else that was currently popular. It was a coveted job because of the high level of social visibility.

The mall was *the* place to hang out with your friends. When you worked there, before long everybody you knew would stop in, sometimes to shop, sometimes just to say hello.

For many kids, it was as much a social opportunity as it was a first job.

The manager, Marta, enjoyed working with the kids, but it was always a challenge keeping them focused. Right from the start, however, Carly seemed different.

Although she had no previous sales skill and, in fact, this was her very first real job, Carly learned quickly. What made her stand apart, though, was that she never waited for her supervisor to tell her what to do. She stayed busy. She was good at looking around and seeing what needed to be done.

The other kids would do an adequate job at anything you asked them to do. Carly, on the other hand, never waited for someone to ask. Other kids would like to socialize with each other or with friends who stopped by. Not Carly. She would be busy folding the clothes or dusting the displays.

Supervisors found it hard to get the other kids to show up on time, but Carly always came in a little early. The other kids kept a close eye on the clock and were quick to leave on time. Carly would always stay longer.

"What else needs to be done?" she would ask.

In short, Carly was there to work for the company that had hired her. She was cheerful, she hustled, and she volunteered. Her strategy, taught to her by her parents, was simple:

"Do more than people expect."

When summer was over, the job was over for the students. Except Carly. The manager, Marta, had already asked Carly if she would like to continue to work part time after school started.

She also mentioned to Carly that the company would have openings in The Gap management training program after Carly graduated. Carly was thrilled.

Did the other kids get the same chance? No way. Why would they? This type of worker is always looking for work. Next summer would bring a fresh batch.

Carly will go far. She has learned to contribute more.

The earlier-mentioned ideas are simple, and they work. Yet they work best when we use them as a philosophy rather than as a strategy. Without the *spirit* of contribution, mere strategies are shallow and self-serving.

We want our children to develop generous, giving hearts. To give without the thought of return is the best mind set—a sign of a truly mature person.

Summary.

Life dissatisfies many people with what it has given them. It is usually a contribution problem.

If you contribute sparingly, then life will reward you sparingly. If you contribute abundantly, then life will reward you abundantly.

Let's inspire our children to give first. To give more. To try harder. Get in earlier. Stay later. Work faster. Smile more. Contribute more kind words. More good ideas. More respect. More effort. More enthusiasm, more hustle.

Do this and they will experience the joy and the rewards of contribution!

Would you like to develop a Rock Solid Parenting philosophy? Receive the free Rock Solid Kids Newsletter! Sign up at www.rocksolidkids.com/newsletter.

Contribution Exercises

Note: Not all exercises are appropriate for all ages; choose the ones best suited for your child's age and experience level.

Week #1

1. My child is:	☐ A big contributor
	☐ An okay contributor
	☐ Not a very good contributor

2. Describe a situation where your child has been a good contributor:

3. Describe a situation where your child's contribution skills need some work:

4. When I was growing up, my family taught me to believe in: (check one)	☐ Abundance
	☐ Scarcity

5. List some reasons why it would be important to believe in abundance:	1.
	2.
	3.
	4.
	5.

6. Reread the "Contribution" chapter. List here any additional thoughts, ideas, or action steps that occur to you:

☐ Check here when you have completed all Week #1 Exercises.

Date:

Week #2

1. Choose an activity for you and your child to use as an exercise in contribution. Select one from the following list or choose one of your own:	☐ Visit sick people in the hospital
	☐ Volunteer to help an elderly neighbor with lawn chores
	☐ Serve together on a committee at your church
	☐ Raise money for a charitable cause
	☐ Other

2. Describe the contribution you and your child will make. Include specific plans, such as days, times, etc.

3. Check here when you and your child have committed to this contribution:

☐ Parent

☐ Child

4. Begin your contribution activity. Describe your beginning action steps and your child's response to them:

5. Reread the "Contribution" chapter. List here any additional thoughts, ideas, or action steps that occur to you:

☐ Check here when you have completed all Week #2 Exercises.

Date:

Week #3

1. Describe your contribution activities up to this point:

2. What has your child's reaction been so far?

3. With your child, review the concept "Contribute First." Discuss ways you can use this concept in your current contribution exercise:

4. Improve your contribution by committing yourself to at least one of the "Contribute First" action steps. Put a check mark by the step you have chosen.

5. Reread the "Contribution" chapter. List here any additional thoughts, ideas, or action steps that occur to you:

☐ Check here when you have completed all Week #3 Exercises.

Date:

Week #4

1. You are now at least three weeks into your contribution exercise. Describe how the experience has gone for both you and your child.

2. With your child, review the concept "Contribute More." Discuss ways you can use this concept in your current contribution exercise.

3. Improve your contribution by committing yourself to at least one of the "Contribute More" action steps. Put a check mark by the step you have chosen.

4. With your child, take a little tour of your town. Point out to your child examples of abundance and examples of scarcity. Discuss with your child the importance of believing in abundance. List any observations your child has made about abundance and scarcity:

5. Rehearse the following questions with your child:	1. "How can I help?"
	2. "What else can I do for you?"
	3. "What else needs to be done?"

6. List some situations where your child can improve her contribution skills by asking the questions in #5:

7. Role-play or rehearse, asking the questions in #5. Give positive responses when you find your child actually using the questions in a real situation.

8. In any contribution situation, we can also improve our contribution by improving our personal skills. Discuss the following ways to improve your contribution. Now have your child check the activities in the list that she is ready to implement.	☐ More effort
	☐ Increased enthusiasm
	☐ Better hustle
	☐ Ask for more responsibility
	☐ Smile more
	☐ Volunteer for additional activities
	☐ Show more respect

9. Reread the "Contribution" chapter. List here any additional thoughts, ideas, or action steps that occur to you:

☐ Check here when you have completed all Week #4 Exercises.

Date:

10. Go back and reread the previous chapter, "Courage," the notes you took, and the commitments you made in the Exercise segment. List here any thoughts or questions that you have:

Great job, parents! You have already helped your child develop some important skills. You are ready to move on to the next chapter!

Put the "Back Yard" Back in Your Kids

When I was a kid (and not that long ago, either!), wherever I went, I would see other kids playing outdoors: pickup baseball games, back yard games, riding bikes, touch football—things like that.

But have you noticed that you don't see too much of this going on anymore? Kids today are more accustomed to being entertained passively. Electronics, video games, and television have really made it difficult for our children to maintain fit, healthy lifestyles.

It's ironic that physical fitness has declined so much in recent years. We live in a time when there are more fitness information, more equipment, and more organized activities than ever before.

Yet the fitness level of our children may still be getting worse and worse.

Kids were born to run and jump and play, to throw things and play catch, to hide behind trees and jump over logs, and do all those high-energy things. So why are too many of today's kids so sedentary? And what price are they paying for such lethargy?

Without Health, You Have Nothing

Everything starts with good health. Without it, you have nothing. Even if you have a fine family, career success, and a wonderful social life.

If you take care of your body, it should serve you for about 100 years. If you neglect your health, you will be a mess by age thirty. Children must be taught that a fit, healthy lifestyle is the accumulation of good habits.

There are three components to a physical fitness program:
- Exercise, of course, is the first.
- The second part is Nutrition.
- The third part is Hygiene and Grooming.

All three areas must be addressed if your children are to have the fit, healthy lifestyle they deserve.

So let's get started!

Begin with a review of your children's current level of physical fitness. Are they active? Or are they developing a "couch-potato" lifestyle?

If they are active and fit, congratulations! You just need to keep them active. As they get older, sometimes even active kids may have a tough time going from organized activities (e.g., soccer, T-ball) to exercise/fitness activities (e.g., running, biking, lifting weights). It's important that they make this transition.

As they become older, it is less likely that they will be on a soccer team and more likely that they will have to develop their own exercise regimens.

Coach-Potato Kids

If you do have a "couch potato" on your hands (or on your couch!), that's okay. It's not too late! It just means that it's time to get started.

What are the symptoms of a child who is out of shape? Often he is lethargic and sluggish. He expresses his feelings of tiredness, boredom, and lack of energy. He moves slowly. He feels discomfort when doing any physical activity for a sustained amount of time.

Take a good look at your child. Can he move quickly when the situation calls for it? Does he seem agile, coordinated? How is his muscle tone? His waistline?

Some children aren't as fit as they should be because they haven't been successful in team activities. Does your child enjoy team activities like hockey, basketball, or baseball? Is she active in school sports? Or has she not quite found her place in those activities? If you find that your daughter didn't like being on the T-ball team or on the soccer team, that's a signal that she may be more suited to individual activities.

Lots of kids don't feel comfortable doing team sports. It's not necessary to force them into group activities. There are a zillion other things they can do!

The problem with some of these team activities is that they are performance based, and they are competitive. If your child isn't confident physically, then it will be difficult for her to enjoy this level of intensity.

Competitive activities are fine for some kids. However, kids who don't enjoy team sports should be given the opportunity to pursue individual activities, where the only goal is fitness and enjoyment!

If your child is less active than she should be, we need to roll up our sleeves and get to work. We need to get moving—literally! But don't worry! You don't need to be a fitness expert to help your child begin.

We begin with a regimen that uses the large muscle groups— your child's legs, arms, and torso. The activity must cause her heartbeat to increase. In other words, aerobic activity!

We want that activity to cause kids to exert themselves at a moderate level of intensity from thirty to sixty minutes. Biking, hiking, walking, swimming … these are all good examples of this type of exercise.

Fitness walking is one of the easiest ways to start. Virtually anybody can do this user-friendly and effective form of exercise. It doesn't require any particular skill or a certain fitness level before you begin. It's easy on the muscles and the joints. No equipment is required, except a good pair of shoes. You can walk in your own neighborhood or go to a park. You can add variety to your walking sessions by going over different routes.

Jogging gets all the attention. But it's hard on the joints. And if you are not in shape already, then it's hard to run long enough to receive any conditioning benefit at all. You get too tired, too soon! And did you know that walking a certain distance burns the same number of calories as running that same distance?

To start, I suggest you make a commitment with your child to go for a brisk walk for fifteen minutes, three times per week. Walk at a moderately quick pace—as if you are going somewhere and trying to be on time. Walk with good posture—chin, chest, and shoulders held high. Keep your muscles loose. Swing your arms. Your left foot and right arm should be moving forward just when your right foot and left arm are moving backward.

Make these three weekly sessions a priority in the family schedule. Look carefully at your schedule to find times that don't conflict with other activities. Once you have established a schedule, stick with it! If you happen to miss a workout, then make it up the next day!

After just thirty days, here is what you will see:
1. Better muscle tone
2. Increased stamina
3. A healthier look on your child's face
4. An improved mental attitude!

At this point, you might move up to a slightly more challenging level of intensity. You can adjust the time that you spend walking, the pace you keep, or the frequency of your workouts. *But remember, all increases must be gradual!*

It's consistency that counts, not intensity! At first, we are trying to instill the habit of exercise but not so much that we overwhelm your children with a difficult regimen.

Try to make exercise a fun experience for your children. At first, you're not trying to benefit from the *walking* as much as you are trying to build an *appreciation of the exertion.*

Exercise is funny. When you don't do it often, it really feels lousy. But when you get started and stick with it, it feels great. So much so, you don't want to quit.

Are You Coming Across as General Patton?

It follows that as you learn to adopt "Rock-Solid" kid skills, you also become a "Rock-Solid" parent. That means your role is to encourage your child by using positive reinforcement.

At times, your kids may be doing things with less enthusiasm than you would like. You might have the impulse to criticize when they are not trying very hard. Resist this urge!

Kids always gravitate toward approval. They want attention. Be sure *not* to give attention to the negative. That will only serve to discourage them. They will feel that your fitness program is just like every other activity they have tried and abandoned. You want to ignore the negative and pour lavish praise upon every effort, upon every approximation of success!

"Rock-Solid" parents must learn to be "good-finders." Look for the one little glimmer of positive effort and pounce on it!

Mrs. Smithers tried this approach with her nine-year-old son, Alex. When she began focusing on physical fitness, she would say things like, "Alex, I was so proud of you for the way you hustled during your walk today! I know you were tired from school, but you handled it so well!"

It's hard to start an exercise program. But it's fairly easy to stick with it if you:

1. Start slowly.
2. Remain consistent.
3. Gradually increase the intensity.

You will soon begin to see a payoff for your efforts—a fit healthy child!

The Basics of Nutrition

The second part of our physical fitness regimen is Nutrition. I'm not a nutrition expert. But, good news! You don't have to be an expert to eat right. Nutrition, in fact, is pretty simple. Here are the basics:

- Make sure that your kids have a balance of the four basic food groups: proteins, carbohydrates, fats, and sugars.
- You want your child to eat the right number of calories each day. Consult a calorie chart to find the correct intake level based on age and weight. Stick to this calorie limit in your meal preparation.
- No more than one-third of your child's calories should come from fat. Just read the food labels to get this information. For example, a food product might have 100 calories. You see that thirty of the calories are fat calories. This is probably a good food choice! Pick up another food product. It also has

100 calories. But this time, fifty-five of them are from fat. Drop it and run!

- Most kids (and adults) are seriously dehydrated. Eight to ten glasses of water per day are necessary—just to replace water lost! Juice, soda, milk, and other beverages don't count! I know—it sounds impossible to drink that much water. Until you start. When you do, you'll find out how great you feel. With the right amount of water in your system, your energy practically doubles. Remember thirst does *not* tell you whether you need water!

- If you ate exactly the right foods and if the vitamin content was not depleted by preservatives, then you wouldn't need a supplement. But how many of us can say we eat a diet like that? Give your kids a good quality multiple-vitamin every day.

I suggest that you start by looking in the refrigerator. Look in the cupboard. Food content labels are now much more user friendly. Read a few. What is the fat content of some foods that your child eats regularly? You might be surprised at how unhealthy some foods are—even ones that have healthy-looking labels or claim to be low fat!

If your child's level of nutrition is not quite what it should be, I don't recommend that you completely overhaul the whole family cooking and grocery-buying process immediately. But I would suggest that you get started right away. Begin by making one or two healthy substitutions each week.

There are lots of low-fat, low-calorie alternatives to foods that you are eating right now. Try a few of them. Some taste so good, you can't tell them apart from their high-fat counterparts.

Gradually increase the amount of fresh fruit and vegetables in the family diet. Avoid some processed foods that may have crept into your grocery cart. Whenever possible, look for foods in their natural states.

Speaking of processed foods, have you seen what they serve for school lunches? I find it incredible that kids leave health class, where they are taught good nutrition, and go to a school lunch that would embarrass the worst fast-food restaurant.

You can avoid this nutritional disaster area by packing a healthy lunch for your child each day. There are tons of healthy things you can pack!

I don't think that you need to entirely cut out fast foods and snack foods from your child's menu. But those things should be viewed as occasional treats—not daily staples!

Our final physical-fitness component is hygiene and grooming. A carefully groomed appearance is a sign of a healthy self-image. Appearances do count!

One father I know, Mr. Brothers, conducts a brief and somewhat humorous "inspection" each morning before Tyler and Dawn leave the house. Teeth brushed? Face washed and hair combed? Nails trimmed and cleaned? Clothes cleaned and pressed? He throws in a little positive reinforcement, like, "Tyler, you look great! I especially like the way you cleaned your fingernails! Dawn, you did a super job getting your clothes ready! Okay, off you go!"

Summary.

It's important that physical fitness habits are established early. Consider for a minute just how hard it is to change these habits when you are older. If you can reach your children with this message at age four or five, it's so much easier than it is later on.

And remember to keep it fun!

Physical Fitness Exercises

Note: Not all exercises are appropriate for all ages; choose the ones best suited for your child's age and experience level.

Week #1

1. My child is:	☐ Very fit, physically
	☐ Somewhat fit
	☐ A couch potato

2. My child tends to like:	☐ Team sports
	☐ Individual sports
	☐ No sports at all

3. Put a check beside any of the following activities that your child enjoys or might enjoy:	☐ Exercise walking
	☐ Swimming
	☐ Jogging
	☐ Biking
	☐ Soccer
	☐ Basketball
	☐ Rollerblading

4. Next conduct a "test" with one of the checked activities. Measure how long your child can continuously perform without having to stop. Check the appropriate box:	ACTIVITY:
	☐ 3 to 5 minutes
	☐ 5 to 15 minutes
	☐ 15 to 30 minutes
	☐ 30 or more minutes

5. Reread the "Physical Fitness" chapter. List here any additional thoughts, ideas, or action steps that occur to you:

☐ Check when you have completed all Week #1 Exercises.

Date:

Week #2

1. Continue with the physical fitness activity you began last week. Later it will be okay to switch activities, but for right now, as we try to build some basic fitness habits, stick to the same one. Try to very gradually increase the time your child is participating.

☐ Check here when your child, with your assistance, has completed three sessions.

2. Currently, our family's nutrition habits are ...	☐ Great
	☐ So-so
	☐ Not so good

3. Take a look in your refrigerator and cupboards. What's in there? List the healthy foods you find:	1.
	2.
	3.
	4.
	5.
	6.

4. Now, list some of the foods eaten regularly by your family that are not so healthy …	1.
	2.
	3.
	4.
	5.
	6.

5. Reread the "Physical Fitness" chapter. List here any additional thoughts, ideas, or action steps that occur to you:

| 1. |
| 2. |
| 3. |

☐ Check here when you have completed all Week #2 Exercises.

Date:

Week #3

1. Continue with the physical-fitness activity you began in Week #1. Again try to gradually increase the amount of time your child is participating. Use positive reinforcement to encourage your child to persist.

☐ Check here when your child, with your assistance, has completed three sessions.

2. Here is a list of healthy meal choices. Put a check beside those that your family enjoys or might enjoy:	☐ Fresh fruits and vegetables
	☐ Lean cuts of meat
	☐ Salads
	☐ Pasta and potatoes
	☐ Grains, cereals, and nuts

3. Here is a list of not-so-healthy choices. Put a check beside those that you might eliminate or reduce in your family's diet:	☐ Fried foods
	☐ Heavily processed foods
	☐ High-calorie desserts
	☐ Soda pop
	☐ Red meat

4. Now consider some healthy substitutions that you might make on grocery-shopping day. Remember, it is best to gradually improve your family's diet.	Before, I bought …
	Now, I will buy …
	Before, I bought …
	Now, I will buy …
	Before, I bought …
	Now, I will buy …
	Before, I bought …
	Now, I will buy …

5. At the grocery store, choose an age-appropriate multiple-vitamin for your family and begin serving it each day.
☐ Check here when you have begun serving the multiple-vitamin.

6. Reread the "Physical Fitness" chapter. List here any additional thoughts, ideas, or action steps that occur to you:

☐ Check here when you have completed all Week #3 Exercises.

Date:

Week #4

1. Continue with the physical fitness activity you began in Week #1. Again try to gradually increase the time your child is participating.

☐ Check here when your child, with your assistance, has completed three sessions.

| 2. Conduct the same test you conducted in Week #1. Measure how long your child can continuously participate in the chosen activity. Measure the results here: | In Week #1, my child could participate for _____ minutes. |
| | Now, in Week #4, she can participate for _____ minutes. |

3. When it comes to your family's new commitment to physical fitness, describe here your child's progress, attitudes, and efforts:

4. Check your child's water intake. It is recommended that a child drink eight servings of water per day (serving size will depend on the age of your child). How many servings of water does your child now take?	☐ 1 to 2
	☐ 3 to 5
	☐ 5 to 8

5. List here some ways that you might be able to increase your child's water intake.	1.
	2.
	3.

6. Good grooming habits are an important part of your child's physical fitness. Is your child:	☐ Well groomed?
	☐ Somewhat well groomed?
	☐ Not very well groomed?

7. Describe your grooming expectations for your child:	1.
	2.
	3.
	4.

8. Describe the "coaching steps" that will be necessary to teach your child to fulfill these expectations:	1. 2. 3. 4.

9. Regular "grooming inspections" with positive feedback are important to this process. Describe here your "grooming-inspection" system:

☐ Check here when you have completed at least three "grooming inspections."

10. Reread the "Physical Fitness" chapter. List here any additional thoughts, ideas, or action steps that occur to you:	1. 2. 3. 4.

☐ Check here when you have completed all Week #4 Exercises.

Date:

Bravo, "Rock-Solid" parents! By completing these physical-fitness exercises, you will have already affected your child's fitness level in a powerful way.

Now, just stick with it. Build on these initial successes and turn them into lifetime habits!

Foundation Stone Eleven: Responsibility

Empowering Your Child to "Pay Her Own Way"

Mary grows up thinking, "Who will help me? When will somebody do something for me? Will the government help me? Or some other institution?"

Craig grows up thinking, "I'll manage, thank you very much. You don't have to worry about me. I can pay my own way."

So these two people grew up with the same opportunities yet with very different ideas about personal responsibility.

We are fortunate to live in a free country. It was founded on the idea of self-reliance and personal responsibility. Because we have personal freedom, it's our responsibility to create the kind of life we want.

As "Rock-Solid" parents, we want our children to grow up to be responsible for themselves. This includes taking responsibility for their actions, commitments, outcomes, and decisions. In effect, to pay their own way.

When your child was born, you assumed full responsibility for her. Over the next twenty years, your job, your responsibility, is to gradually turn that *responsibility* over to her.

The "Responsibility Model"

Teaching your child to be responsible takes time and attention from you. Every bit of responsibility you give your child has to come with a tremendous amount of instruction and supervision. You must be prepared to teach, remind, and inspect—over and over, a zillion times. What's more, you must be prepared to do this without becoming frustrated or resentful.

The following is a model that you can follow to teach your child how to handle responsibility:

1. Teach your child what you expect and how to meet those expectations.

2. Give him a little space to try.

3. Inspect and provide constructive feedback.

4. If your child's efforts were successful, great. Just continue with Step #3. If your child's results weren't quite successful, then you just need to increase your coaching and the number of times you give positive feedback.

(Note: Initial failure doesn't mean you take away the responsibility. It just means you need a little more teaching and more frequent feedback.)

Mrs. Morgan used the Responsibility Model when the Morgan family brought home a new puppy. Jessica, eight, was tremendously excited. She said, "Mom, can I be the one to take care of the puppy?" Mom was hesitant. Jessica had never handled a responsibility like this before.

In fact, she had not been very successful at handling smaller responsibilities. Still, Mom realized that this was an opportunity to teach Jessica some responsibility skills.

Mom said, "Okay. Here's what you will have to do. Puppy needs food and fresh water each morning. That means you will have to get up about five minutes earlier. Also, when you get home from school, she will need more fresh water. You'll have to remember to do this before you go outside to play. She will also need some more food at night before you go to bed."

The next day, Mom watched to see what would happen. Jessica got up early and fed the puppy. But after school, she came home, dropped off her books, and headed out the door to play. Mom gently reminded Jessica to feed the dog. Later that night, without being reminded, Jessica filled the puppy's dish.

Each day, Mom must observe Jessica's behavior and be ready to step in with reminders. It may be a long time until Jessica is ready to do these tasks without some help from Mom.

Sound like a lot of work? It is! Would it be easier to do it yourself? Of course! Often, the commitment it takes to teach a child how to be responsible surprises many parents. They become frustrated and stop trying.

Yet if Mom gets frustrated and takes over Jessica's responsibilities, what does Jessica learn?

I was talking with a man I know named Clark. Clark was telling me that he had a lot of lawns to cut and that it was taking a great deal of his time.

I seemed to remember that Clark had his teenage son helping him. I said, "I thought you had your son, Ryan, helping you."

Clark said, "You are right. I did. But Ryan always did a poor job. He would always forget to cut the grass. When he did remember, he usually did a sloppy job. I couldn't count on him."

I said, "Did you teach Ryan what you expected? Did you pop in from time to time to see how he was doing?"

Clark seemed surprised, "Ryan's fifteen years old. Can't he cut a few lawns without me looking over his shoulder?"

Maybe. But in my experience, people will never do their best in handling their responsibilities without instruction, a clear set of expectations, and feedback.

Maybe you don't believe this. If you feel the way Clark did, then let me ask you, "How do you do if your boss occasionally inspects your work?" What would happen if he increased the frequency of the inspections? Would you pay a little more attention to the quality of your work? Most of us would.

What if he decreased the frequency of the inspections or stopped them altogether? Are you confident that you could maintain the same quality and quantity of work?

For most of us, the answer is "No." It is human nature for us to perform at a higher level when we know that others will inspect our work. In time, for most of us, the quality of that work would slip if we got no feedback.

Clark didn't feel the need to provide that level of instruction and supervision. So he became frustrated and quit. Too bad. He missed a great opportunity to teach.

If you skip steps in the Responsibility Model, then chances are that your child won't be able to effectively handle his responsibility. This leads to resentment from both you and your child.

Even at an early age, our children begin to make choices and commitments. The privilege of choosing requires responsibility.

I remember when my son Ian joined his first band. After months of practice, the band finally landed its first playing job. The band members were so excited.

In the middle of telling Renee and me the details, Ian stopped abruptly. A crushed look came over his face. Right then, he remembered that he had already committed to helping me at an overnight training session at the Karate school.

On his own, without any prompting from us, Ian made the phone calls to his band members, saying that he couldn't play. Ian knew that his responsibility was to the first person that he'd made a commitment to. Renee and I were sad that he had to miss his music, but we were pleased that he had acted responsibly.

Outcomes

School provides lots of opportunities to teach responsibility. For most kids, the grades they receive are their first performance indicators. That's where we could use the Responsibility Model.

Trevor was in the fifth grade. On his previous report card, the only grades were Satisfactory and Unsatisfactory. Now, for the first time, Trevor's report card contained letter grades. Unfortunately, the results weren't too good.

Trevor had this conversation with his Dad:

Dad: "Trevor, I'm not too happy with this report card."

Trevor: "But, Dad, the teacher doesn't like me. None of the kids like her. She's mean!"

Dad: "I'm afraid you aren't accepting responsibility. You're trying to blame others for your failure. Those grades are your responsibility. Now let's talk about how you could do better."

Trevor's dad was smart. He didn't let Trevor make excuses. He wasn't trying to blame him for bad grades. He was just trying to get him to assume responsibility for them.

If Trevor's dad were to follow the Responsibility Model, he might say something like this:

"Trevor, I'm pretty sure you can maintain a 'B' average. This is what I expect from you. Let's try to organize your study times to make sure that you're devoting enough time to your homework. Then, when I get home from work, we'll take a look at your assignments. If they look okay, we'll go out back and shoot some baskets. If your assignments need a little work, I'll make some suggestions, and you can work on them right then."

Of course, Trevor's dad now needs to follow through. It is his ability to keep his commitment that will determine whether Trevor integrates this concept into his life.

Privileges

All kids want privileges. All privileges carry responsibilities. For example, if you have the privilege of using the car, then you are responsible for following the rules of the road.

If your privilege is going to the movies with a friend, then you are responsible for your conduct and your curfew as well as any other special instructions you might receive from Mom and Dad.

We have the privilege of living in a free country. That privilege definitely requires certain acts of responsible behavior on our part. We have the responsibility of following the laws of our country. We must make ourselves available for our country if it drafts us into service. We must do anything else we can to protect the liberty that we all enjoy. These are responsibilities that we assume when we have the privilege of living in a country that affords us liberty and freedom of choice.

Summary.

It's a huge mistake to assume that our children will grow up to be responsible adults without a huge amount of coaching.

It's a lot of hard work. But it's also one of the most enriching, rewarding experiences that can take place between a parent and child. You will be so proud when you see your child grow up to be a responsible adult!

So parents, be diligent. Use the model. Don't become frustrated or give up. Stick with it, and your child will learn to handle all types of responsibility effectively!

Responsibility Exercises

Note: Not all exercises are appropriate for all ages; choose the ones best suited for your child's age and experience level.

Week #1

1. My child's sense of responsibility is …	☐ Great
	☐ Fair
	☐ Not so good

2. An example of a time when my child handled responsibility effectively would be:

3. An example of a time when my child did not handle responsibility effectively would be:

4. Reread the "Responsibility" chapter. List here any additional thoughts, ideas, or action steps that occur to you:

☐ Check here when you have completed all Week #1 Exercises.
Date:

Week #2

1. List three times when your child handled responsibility effectively. In each situation, describe the type of support and instruction that you provided:	1. Responsibility my child handled effectively:
	Support and instruction I provided:
	2. Responsibility my child handled effectively:
	Support and instruction I provided:
	3. Responsibility my child handled effectively:
	Support and instruction I provided:

2. Now let's look at some situations where my child did not handle responsibility effectively and see if we can identify some areas of support and instruction I could have provided:	1. Responsibility my child did not handle effectively:
	Support and instruction I could have/should have provided:
	2. Responsibility my child did not handle effectively:
	Support and instruction I could have/should have provided:
	3. Responsibility my child did not handle effectively:
	Support and instruction I could have/should have provided:

3. Reread the "Responsibility" chapter. List here any additional thoughts, ideas, or action steps that occur to you:

☐ Check here when you have completed all Week #2 Exercises.

Date:

<u>Week #3</u>

1. This week, we will focus on the Responsibility Model. Go back to the "Responsibility" chapter and reread the section entitled, "The Responsibility Model."
☐ Check here when you have reread this important segment.

2. Now identify a situation where you can put the "Responsibility Model" to the test. Begin by listing some potential areas of responsibility for your child:	1.
	2.
	3.
	4.
	5.

3. Now select one of the ideas for your first exercise in the "Responsibility Model."
The area I choose is:

4. Let's follow the "Responsibility Model:"	The responsibility will be:
	What I expect is:
	1.
	2.
	3.
	4.
	5.

5. Now describe the type of support, instruction, and feedback you will provide:

6. Meet with your child and describe the responsibility you will be giving her. Explain in detail your expectations and the type of support that can be expected from you. Describe here your child's response to the meeting here:

7. Reread the "Responsibility" chapter. List here any additional thoughts, ideas, or action steps that occur to you:

☐ Check here when you have completed all Week #3 Exercises.

Date:

Week #4

1. As you follow through with your child's responsibility assignment, describe the experience here:

2. So far, my child's efforts in this area have been:	☐ Hugely successful
	☐ Somewhat successful
	☐ Not too successful

3. If your results are hugely successful, congratulations! If they are less successful, then just back up a bit and provide some extra coaching. List here some extra coaching steps that will help your child deal more successfully with this responsibility:	1.
	2.
	3.

4. Meet with your child and discuss the concept of "Privilege" and the concept of "Responsibility." Explain that all privileges depend on responsibilities being handled effectively. List here some of your child's privileges and the responsibilities that accompany them:	1. Privilege One:
	Corresponding responsibility:
	2. Privilege Two:
	Corresponding responsibility:
	3. Privilege Three:
	Corresponding responsibility:

| 5. Now discuss some of your child's potential future privileges and the responsibilities that will go along with them: | 1. Future privilege: |
| | *Corresponding responsibility:* |

	2. Future privilege:
	Corresponding responsibility:
	3. Future privilege:
	Corresponding responsibility:

6. Reread the "Responsibility" chapter. List here any additional thoughts, ideas, or action steps that occur to you:

☐ Check here when you have completed all Week #4 Exercises.

Date:

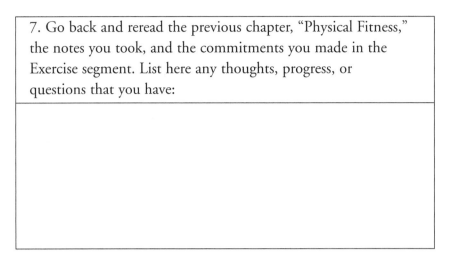

7. Go back and reread the previous chapter, "Physical Fitness," the notes you took, and the commitments you made in the Exercise segment. List here any thoughts, progress, or questions that you have:

Well, it is a lot of hard work to teach a child responsibility, isn't it? But remember, it's a lot more work to raise a child who can't effectively handle responsibility! You are to be congratulated for making it this far. I wish every child had a parent as committed as you are. Awesome job!

Keep your commitment to being a Rock Solid Parent - sign up for Keith Hafner's Free Rock Solid Kids Newsletter!
Visit www.rocksolidkids.com/newsletter to sign up!

Foundation Stone Twelve: Persistence

Can Your Child Stick It Out?

There was a time when the world moved at a much slower pace. People went for walks, made their own clothes, put together jigsaw puzzles, made meals from scratch, and read Shakespeare. In those days, it was more natural for people to be persistent. People just assumed that things would take time.

Today's world, however, moves at a much more rapid pace. Now, with the Internet, CNN, *USA Today*, microwaved food, and air travel, we have become a people who demand immediate gratification. We have lost some of our ability to be persistent.

Although the world has changed in many ways, it's still the same in one important way: Despite today's frenetic pace, the world still gives up its rewards slowly. That means you must have a plan, a course of action—and stick with it.

Success does a "gut check" in persistence. It demands not only skill and talent. Success requires that you use your skill and talent applied to a specific course of action. Never forget, you must pass through a waiting period before the course opens up its rewards. It's the key to the whole effort. Huge profits and rewards await those who stick it out.

Even now, we still see some people earning college degrees, becoming Eagle Scouts, and earning black belts—while others accomplish very little. They are good at starting things but not so good at seeing them through to completion.

Here's how accomplishment works:

1. *The Excitement Phase*: When you begin, you get an initial rush of fun and satisfaction. The prospect of beginning a new activity is exciting. You feel motivated in this early stage; you make quick progress as you master basic skills.

2. *The Persistence Phase*: After a time, the initial excitement wears off, and satisfaction diminishes. The activity is not new anymore, not quite so easy, and not quite so much fun. You begin a long climb with fewer observable results. With little apparent progress, the result is boredom. Boredom is the enemy of persistence. Most people quit during this step.

3. *The Reward Phase*: As you near completion, the excitement returns. You experience a renewed sense of commitment. You can finally see the finish line! Big rewards await those who persist. Nothing feels better than completing a difficult task!

The challenge lies in Step 2, the Persistence Phase. This is why persistence is so important for our children.

Never forget, they will not experience any meaningful success unless they become experts at handling Step 2!

I learned the value of persistence when I was a kid, in my early martial arts days. I always admired the skills of the more expert martial arts masters. Still, I began to notice something that surprised me. No matter how talented they were, most of these great practitioners would end up quitting their study of martial arts! They had lost the desire to go further.

Before, I had thought that talent was everything. But I began to see that talent amounts to nothing the minute you quit. I began to understand that to succeed, all I had to do was not quit.

Now when people say to me, "Master Hafner, how did you achieve the 6th Degree Black Belt?" I usually reply, "I just kept showing up. They couldn't get rid of me. So they had to keep promoting me!"

Interestingly, they call the style of martial arts that I have studied and now teach, *Tae Kwon Do Chung Do Kwan. Chung Do Kwan* refers to "The Great Blue Wave." It describes the power of water to gradually wear away the surface of a rock. A perfect model of persistence!

People think talent is the key to achieving big goals. It's not. Instead, it's persistence. Remember what Calvin Coolidge, President of the United States, said:

Nothing in the world can take the place of persistence.

Talent will not; nothing is more common than unsuccessful men with talent.

Genius will not; unrewarded genius is almost a proverb.

Education will not; the world is full of educated derelicts.

Persistence and determination alone are omnipotent. The slogan "press on," has solved and always will solve the problems of the human race.

So again, nothing takes the place of persistence.

In any endeavor, lots of talented people quit. Persistent people hang around and succeed. So the quitters end up thinking that the persistent "must have more talent"!

How to Teach Persistence

To teach your child persistence, you must get him to increase the time he spends on the specific tasks important to him. By steadily and gradually increasing the time, in fact, anyone can improve his persistence.

Part of the challenge with teaching kids to be persistent is that they just haven't lived long enough to understand the way that time unfolds. That's okay, "Rock-Solid" parents! That's why we must learn to teach these skills!

Keep these four key points in mind:

1. To overcome discouragement in completing a task, you must understand that a natural part of the learning process is the "plateau." This occurs during Step 2, the "Persistence Phase." Although you are continuing in your efforts, it feels like you are not making progress.

The plateau is a necessary part of the learning process! Your child will handle plateaus better when he understands that they are a normal part of the learning process.

My son Ian is now an accomplished guitar player. When he first began playing, it came to him easily. He mastered the beginning chords and was soon playing complete songs. It was only a matter of time before he had formed a band and was performing in front of small audiences.

Sometime later, Ian came to me and said, "Dad, I feel like I'm not making any progress at the guitar. I still practice as much, but I'm not getting any better." Being familiar with the plateau, I encouraged him to stick with it. I assured him that a breakthrough would come soon.

Sure enough, it did. Ian persisted, and his playing advanced to the next level. He now knows that plateaus are inevitable. They are just a temporary delay in the results-getting process.

2. Help your child replace negative self-talk with positive self-talk. Negative self-talk can make your child quit a challenging task despite his intention to finish it.

I've never done anything worth doing without my brain trying to talk me out of it. When the alarm clock goes off in the morning, my brain says, "Why don't you sleep in, just this once?" When it's time to do my workout, my brain says, "Hey, you're really busy.

Maybe you should skip a day." When it comes to persistence, your brain is your worst enemy.

For example, let's say you are running a three-mile race. It's a fine morning, and you are feeling good. At the starting line, your brain strikes up a conversation with you:

Brain: "Hey, this is great. It's going to be easy!"

You: "I know. Let's get started."

You begin running. After about a mile …

Brain: "I thought this was going to be fun. It's not so much fun anymore. Maybe we should take a break."

You: "Be quiet! I'm trying to run."

You persist, huffing and puffing. Soon …

Brain: "You know, your feet are really starting to hurt. You might be doing some serious damage. Why don't we quit? We could go out to breakfast."

You: "I really want to finish. Please pipe down!"

Brain: "Why did you think you could run three miles? You haven't been training all that hard. These other runners are better than you."

You: "Well, I meant to train more."

Brain: "I bet you will next time. Let's quit."

You: "Okay."

Now imagine the same situation. This time, with positive self-talk, it might go something like:

Brain: "Hey, it's getting hot in here. Let's take a br—"

You: "I will persist until I succeed!"

Brain: "Huh? Well, okay, for now."

Later …

Brain: "Enough is enough! Time to qui—"

You: "I will persist until I succeed! I will persist until I succeed! I will persist until I succeed!"

Brain: "Well, I guess you know what you are doing."

You: "I will persist until I succeed! I will persist until I succeed!"

Your Brain falls silent. It gives up. You have won!

Your child must understand the voice and know that it is lying. He must be prepared to replace it with positive self-talk.

3. Learning to persist through physical fatigue teaches your child how to handle discouragement in completing tasks. If your child has a low level of physical endurance, then he'll find it difficult to fight through periods of discouragement. Your child must learn how to persist in a long, slow process like running or swimming. That way, he learns how to control both his mind and body.

When Pat began swimming, she had good technique and quickly mastered the basics. When it came time to swim laps, however, she could only swim a couple of lengths before she had to stop. Her teacher didn't know if her efforts were physically exhausting her, or if she was simply not used to pushing herself. However, he continued to encourage her, and she made steady progress in her endurance. As her strength grew, so did her ability to push herself beyond her earlier limits.

Pat's parents used "Rock-Solid" thinking and began to teach her how she could push herself in other areas, too. Her schoolwork began to improve, and so did her self-esteem!

4. Teach your child that all his commitments (both to others and himself) must be honored.

Melissa begged her parents to join the local soccer team. It meant participating twice per week for ten weeks. Melissa had never stuck out a commitment of that length before.

"Okay," Dad said, "But you've got to fulfill your obligation to the team. Even if you get discouraged, you have to complete the season." Melissa agreed.

Sure enough, after about five weeks, the initial excitement had worn off. The weather was turning cold, and Melissa began to complain about having to go to soccer. "Myra's parents don't make her go if she doesn't feel like it!" she complained.

But Mom and Dad held firm. They said, "Honey, you are responsible for this commitment. You must finish the season." Melissa reluctantly complied.

By the end of the season, Melissa's skills had continued to develop, and she began to feel like an important part of the team. Her persistence rewarded her by restoring her initial enthusiasm, teaching her a valuable lesson about keeping commitments.

Melissa's parents were smart. Because they insisted Melissa be persistent, they taught her not to give up when she became discouraged.

Now let's think about Melissa's friend, Myra, for a minute. Her parents did let her quit. What did they teach her about persistence? What will happen next time a commitment becomes difficult for Myra?

As your child matures, you must be ready to challenge him with longer projects and activities. *Sesame Street*-type activities are fine when your child is three or four. After that, it's time to move on.

Right now, many of your child's current activities may be short. That's okay; they serve a purpose, too. Except it may be time to look for a longer-term project.

Eric was only four when his dad enlisted him to help move a large pile of rocks into the field behind the house. It took Eric most of the summer to complete the task.

Each time Dad put on his boots to work in the yard, Eric would put his boots on, too. Dad would start cutting the grass or raking leaves. Eric would start making the long walk across the yard with a rock in each tiny hand.

When Dad would pass nearby with the lawnmower, he would never miss an opportunity to give Eric a big thumbs-up. Eric would set his rocks down, return the sign, pick up his rocks, and resume his work with new energy.

Dad also established a little ritual. Drinking out of the hose in the yard was a privilege reserved only for "guys who can stick things out." Of course, several times during each work session, the "guys who could stick things out" would gather at the hose for a refreshing pause.

Dad also never missed an opportunity to reinforce Eric's newly developing persistence. While he and Eric were washing up for dinner, he would say, in Eric's presence, "Mom, you should have seen Eric today. He must have carried a million rocks. I've never before seen a kid who can stick to a job the way Eric can."

Let's review what Eric's dad did. First, he gave Eric a long-term project. He provided the coaching, the supervision, and the support. He also kept Eric focused and motivated with frequent positive feedback. He also established a powerful picture in Eric's mind—of himself as a "guy who sticks things out, no matter what." This picture will support Eric's persistence for years to come.

When you observe even small amounts of persistence in your child, reinforce these efforts with positive feedback, like:

- "Sammy, I was so proud of the way you finished raking the leaves. You really stuck it out!"
- "You impressed us a lot with the way you completed the basketball season. Grab your coat. Let's celebrate with an ice cream cone!"

Summary.

As with other "Rock-Solid" skills, persistence requires supervision. You can't give your child a long, arduous task and expect her to complete it without coaching, support, and positive reinforcement. Depending on the task, you may have to work alongside your child.

Make it a habit to notice persistence in your child. Reward it. Reinforce it. Remember, even approximations of success are important. They are the seeds out of which persistence grows!

Persistence Exercises

Note: Not all exercises are appropriate for all ages; choose the ones best suited for your child's age and experience level.

Week #1

1. My child has ...	☐ A lot of persistence
	☐ Some persistence
	☐ Very little persistence

2. An example of my child demonstrating persistence:

3. An example of my child needing more persistence:

4. In the past, how have I handled it when my child has wanted to quit something rather than stick it out? Give three examples here:	1.
	2.
	3.

5. Reread the "Persistence" chapter. List here any additional thoughts, ideas, or action steps that occur to you:

☐ Check here when you have completed all Week #1 Exercises.

Date:

Week #2

1. One of the best ways to develop persistence is to challenge your child with a long-term project and let him experience the satisfaction that comes with long-term effort. Select a project from the following list or choose one of your own:	1. Read a book together. Choose a book of challenging length. Work toward completion by breaking it into small sessions. 2. Put together a big jigsaw puzzle. 3. Go to the hobby store and get a model car or ship or some other type of craft project. 4. Find a work project like Eric's dad did on pages 189-190. 5. Other:

Note: Whatever project you choose, remember to keep it fun! Provide lots of gentle coaching and positive reinforcement. Remember that the goal is not to get the project done. The goal is to provide a supportive experience that will help your child develop persistence!

The persistence project I commit to is:

2. Meet with your child and explain the project you will be tackling together. Generate as much excitement for the project as possible. Make it fun!

3. This week, complete three mini-sessions of work on the project.

☐ Check here when you have completed all three.

4. Reread the "Persistence" chapter. List here any additional thoughts, ideas, or action steps that occur to you:

☐ Check here when you have completed all Week #2 Exercises.

Date:

Week #3

1. Continue to work on your persistence project.

☐ Check here when you've completed an additional three sessions.

2. Describe your child's participation in the persistence project. Include any changes that may be occurring from session to session:

<table>
<tr><td colspan="2"></td></tr>
</table>

3. So far, my child's persistence has been …	☐ Awesome
	☐ So-so
	☐ Not so good

4. If you described your child's response as "awesome," list here the type of positive feedback you have been providing:

5. If you described your child's response as "so-so" or "not so good," list some types of feedback and encouragement you could be providing to help your child develop persistence:

6. Your child will be Persistent when she gets control over her "self-talk." Select one of the "Persistence Affirmations" and teach it to your child:	☐ "I will persist until I succeed!"
	☐ "I never quit!"
	☐ "I complete each task I undertake!"

	☐ Other:

7. Teach this affirmation to your child by saying it to her and having her say it back to you.

☐ Check here when you have taught her the affirmation and repeated the exercise several times.

8. Reread the "Persistence" chapter. List here any additional thoughts, ideas, or action steps that occur to you:

☐ Check here when you have completed all Week #3 Exercises.

Date:

Week #4

1. Physical fitness is an important part of developing persistence.

☐ Check here when you are done.

2. My child's physical stamina is:	☐ Great
	☐ Okay
	☐ Not so good

3. If you have checked "okay" or "not so good," review the exercises you did in the "Physical Fitness" chapter and get back on track with physical stamina. It's an important part of persistence!

4. Continue with your persistence exercise.

☐ Check here when you have done at least three more sessions.

5. If your project is nearing completion, congratulations! Remember to congratulate your child and reinforce the experience. Because our persistence training is ongoing, our next project will be:

6. Reinforce the Persistence Affirmation you taught your child last week by including yourself in it. For example, as you work on your persistence project, say, "We persist until we succeed, don't we, Chris!"

☐ Check here when you have used the Persistence Affirmation at least three times.

7. Reread the "Persistence" chapter. List here any additional thoughts, ideas, or action steps that occur to you:

☐ Check here when you have completed all Week #4 Exercises.

Date:

8. Go back and reread the previous chapter, "Responsibility," the notes you took, and the commitments you made in the Exercise segment. List here any thoughts, progress, or questions that you have:

Well done, "Rock-Solid" parents. Remember that it takes Persistence on your part to develop Persistent kids. Stick with these exercises, and you will find your children developing the "stick-to-it-iveness" that will empower them to reach any goal! Take a few minutes right now and review your notes from all previous chapters. Write down three "reminders" to yourself:

| Reminder #1 |
| Reminder #2 |
| Reminder #3 |

Epilogue

Never forget, our kids are our greatest legacy. Sure, we can enjoy great success in other areas of our lives. But we cannot find any to match that of seeing our own children succeed. Best of all, to know, deep down, that we've played a key role.

Remember, though, the clock is running. We only have a few short years to prepare our kids to face not only the world but also themselves.

As this book has shown, however, we don't need lots of fancy theories and "experts" to get the job done. Children of all ages can learn the ideas and strategies found in this book. Even better, any parent can teach them. You don't need any special training, other than what you find in this book. Remember, I have already successfully taught these strategies to kids from all over the world— for years.

It doesn't matter where you live or how much money you make. These strategies worked 100 years ago and will still be working 100 years from now.

Finally, never forget, *You Can't **Not** Teach!* So use the strategies that have worked for successful parents throughout history!

Index

Write Your Success Story and Get a ...

FREE
"Rock-Solid Kids"
T-SHIRT

Have "Rock-Solid Kids" strategies worked for you? Send us your story and we'll send you a free "Rock-Solid Kids" T-shirt. (Please limit your story to a maximum of 200 words.)

T-Shirt Size: ☐ XX Large ☐ X Large
☐ Large ☐ Medium ☐ Small

Send Your Story Via:

Fax: (734) 994-3692
e-mail: khafner@provide.net
Or mail:
Keith Hafner's Karate
214 S. Main Street
Ann Arbor, MI 48104

(Don't forget to tell us your t-shirt size.)

Give the book,
Rock-Solid Kids

Send a gift with life-changing impact. Send *How to Build Rock-Solid Kids* to a family member or friend—or just to yourself. (We'll include a card from you at no extra cost.)

SEND TO: FROM:

Name _____   Name _____

Street _____   Street _____

City _____   City _____

State _____ Zip _____   State _____ Zip _____

Send check for $27.95 ($22.95 plus $5.00 shipping and handling) to:

Keith Hafner's Karate
214 S. Main Street
Ann Arbor, MI 48104

Or fax your order to: (734) 994-3692

☐ Master Card ☐ VISA ☐ Discover Card ☐ American Express

Name _____ Exp. Date _____

Card # _____ Phone _____

Signature_____

Are you ready to become
a Rock Solid Parent?

Visit **100parentingtips.com**
for a **Free** report!